HOW TO
PUBLISH, PROMOTE AND
SELL YOUR BOOK

Compiled and Written by
JOSEPH V. GOODMAN

ADAMS PRESS
30 W. WASHINGTON STREET
CHICAGO, ILLINOIS 60602

This book is typeset in Century Book type, printed on 70# vellum paper, and bound in a kromekote cover.

FIFTH EDITION
1986 Revised

Copyright © 1986 by Adams Press

Previous editions copyright © 1960, 1965, 1970, 1977

LIBRARY OF CONGRESS CATALOG
CARD NUMBER 86-90813

INTERNATIONAL STANDARD BOOK NUMBER
0-910018-01-4

12,000 copies in print

Printed in the United States of America

TABLE OF CONTENTS

(continued on next page)

Introduction

This book was written primarily for the author who plans to publish a book at his own expense and who is interested in learning how he can promote his book and sell as many copies as possible. Much of the material has never appeared in print while other previously printed information has been incorporated in this one volume.

Due to space limitations, it is not possible to include all data that might have been incorporated. In such cases, reference is made to other sources where more complete information can be found. While all data has been checked for accuracy at the time of publication, it is possible that by the time this book is read, changes may have occurred. Addresses may change, companies may go out of business, and policies of firms may be revised. However, it is felt that this book contains much valuable information for the self-publishing author, especially the one with a limited budget.

The author of this book has had over 45 years of experience in the book printing field. He has learned how many small publishers effectively promote their books, and this information is now being passed on to the reader. It is the aim of this book to help the self-publishing author sell and distribute more copies of his book than would otherwise have been possible.

Because of constantly changing prices, the cost for books, subscriptions, etc. may now be outdated. Be sure to write first before sending any orders or money.

Why Should I Publish My Book?

Every author honestly believes that he has written a wonderful book that will be bought and enjoyed by many people if only the public can be informed that such a book exists. He envisions sales in the hundreds of thousands if the book is properly promoted and that the public will rush to the bookstores to buy his book. His enthusiasm may overshadow his good judgment and the book becomes his personal obsession.

The first disappointment comes when a legitimate publisher rejects the manuscript as unacceptable for publication. The publisher has read the manuscript objectively. He is not interested in whether it is a good book—he is interested solely in whether it will sell. He knows that publishing is a hazardous business with only a few best sellers. He also knows that he must sell about 15,000 copies to get over the break even point. Manufacturing and distributing costs are high and the competition is keen. He just can't afford to take the risk.

We are assuming that the book has merit, is well written, and is properly presented to the publisher. Perhaps as high as 50% of the manuscripts are returned because of poor writing style, errors in spelling and grammar, limited appeal subject matter, or a poorly prepared manuscript.

The author covers his disappointment by feeling that the publisher is missing the opportunity of a lifetime. He will give another publisher the "right" to publish his book. But chances are that he will get rejection after rejection, some accompanied by a courteous personal letter; others by a printed form letter.

It seems that publishers will print books authored only by well known personalities in the entertainment or political field or by authors who have already made names for themselves in the literary world. It is almost impossible for the unpublished author to get his book accepted for publication by a legitimate publishing house.

The next step will be to contact one of the so-called "subsidy" publishers, also known as "vanity" publishers. (See special section in this book on "The Truth About Subsidy Publishers.") Chances are that the author will receive a glowing account of how "thrilled" the preliminary reader was while reading the manuscript, together with a handsomely printed brochure describing the many books issued by this publisher under the co-operative publishing plan. He will be advised how much it will cost the author to get a limited number of copies printed, and how much "royalty" the author will be paid for each book sold.

However, if the author will take the time to check with his local Better Business Bureau or the Federal Trade Commission in Washington, D. C., he will soon learn the truth about these subsidy publishers. He will find that few authors (if any) get even a fraction of their original investment back from royalty sales, and that much of the advertising is deceptive (according to the Federal Trade Commission). And so, if he is smart, the author will look around for another method of getting his book into print.

The author may now ask himself the question, "Why do I have to get my book published?" He alone is in a position to answer that question. Perhaps the prestige of getting a book published is the primary answer. He will be elevated in the eyes of his friends and relatives even though not one copy of the book is sold. If he is a doctor, lawyer, teacher, or other professional or trades man, he can enhance his status by being the author of a book in a specialized field. He may find himself in demand as a consultant or expert as a result of the published book. And if he is seeking a new position, the fact that he authored a book on some subject will be given weight in determining his qualifications for the job.

Others can achieve overnight fame in their local community, club, or business by having a book published. It has been worth the investment without any thought of ever recouping the money the author spent in getting the book into print.

Many authors are not interested in prestige or fame that comes with the publication of their book, but still feel that they can sell enough copies to make a profit, with the possibility of additional reprints, or sales rights for magazine, book club, radio and television, or movie adaptation. They want to own all the books they print; they want to sell and distribute the books themselves; and primarily, they want to create a demand for their books through an aggressive promotional campaign.

In all fairness, it must be pointed out that self-published books that earn fat profits for the author are very rare indeed. Many are fortunate to break even, or just suffer a small loss. However, the author has satisfied himself that at least he has tried. There is no more frustrated individual than the author who goes through life with an unpublished manuscript on his desk, always wondering whether he might not have had a best seller had he but spent a few dollars getting his manuscript into book form and before the reading public.

The simplest, quickest, and least expensive method of getting a book into print is to deal with a reliable and experienced printer of books. There are many fine book printers who will print a limited number of copies for a fixed reasonable cost. They make no glowing promises of the sales possibilities of your book. You will get the books expertly printed and bound – the rest is up to you. Whether the author wants to sell his copies, give them away, or donate them to the library is strictly the author's business. The printer's sole interest is to get the book printed in the fastest possible time at the lowest possible cost.

Reprinted from "Writer's Digest" by permission

"I'm so thrilled to meet an author. What do you do for a living?"

Getting Ready for Publication

The fact that you are reading this book is an indication that either you have a manuscript ready for publication or that one is in the process of preparation. Questions may come to mind and an attempt will be made to resolve these problems in this section.

The first step is to visit a local bookstore and browse through the books. Find one that will be similar to what you have in mind and buy it. Take it home and examine it carefully. Note what goes on the front cover and what on the back cover. Open the book and check the first page which is the title page. On back of the title page you will find the copyright page and see what material appears on this page. Also note that the odd numbered pages, 1, 3, 5, 7, etc. are printed on the right hand page, and the even numbered pages, 2, 4, 6, 8, etc. are printed on the left hand page on the backs of the odd numbered pages.

What Size Book Shall I Order? Books ordinarily are printed in three popular sizes. First, there is the 5½x8½ (or 6x9) size, most preferred by self-publishing authors. It is the most economical size for any given number of words. Each page takes approximately 400 words when typeset and is suitable for both paperback and hard covered books. This size book fits easily on a book or library shelf. It is also the recommended size for those preparing their own pages for offset printing.

Then there is the 4¼x7 (or 5x7) size which is the size of paperback books sold by the millions in bookstores, drugstores, and department stores. This size takes from 280 to 300 words to the page when typeset. Lastly, comes the 8½x11 (or 9x12) size. This size is cumbersome to handle and is recommended only for technical books that require large maps, diagrams or illustrations. After analyzing the above data, you will be better able to select the page size for your book.

Paperbacks or Hard Covers: Within the past few years, paperback bound books have reached a peak of popularity never before thought possible. Even the prestige publishers, who at one time turned their backs on producing "soft cover" books, have now entered the paperback field. Most school textbooks have adopted paperback binding.

The reason is simple. Manufacturing costs have soared to the extent that many of the cloth bound books are priced out of reach of the average book buyer. Paperbacks can be produced and sold up to four to six dollars less per book than clothbound books. In addition, paperbacks are lighter in weight and cheaper to mail, easier to handle while traveling, and take up less space on the bookshelf. On the other hand, some libraries still refuse to handle paperback bound books. Hard covered books are preferred as they are more durable and make a more attractive display on the book or library shelf. Some people still feel that a book is not a book unless it is bound in cloth. Authors who wish to satisfy both types of readers can get part of their books in paperback and part in cloth. Thus, it is possible to order 1,000 copies of a book with 750 in paperbacks and 250 in hard clothbound covers. By having a small number of the books bound in hard covers, the author will have some hard covered books available for his own shelf as well as for limited distribution. Not only is there a higher cost for the cloth covers, but there will be an additional expense for the printing of dust jackets and the purchasing of special padded bags for sending the books through the mails.

Typeset vs. Offset Printing: There are two methods by which your book can be printed. First is the traditional typeset method where the printer sets the type from your manuscript and prints the pages. This is normally done on computerized "cold type" photo composition machines that are fast and accurate. By this method you have a choice of various faces of type. Your printer should be able to supply a typeface booklet from which you can make your selection. Or depend on his expertise to make this choice for you.

The other more economical method is to have your book printed by photo offset from "camera ready" pages prepared by the author. This requires the author to type each page just as he wants it to appear. The printer photographs each page exactly as submitted and reproduces it in the book. The printer does no typesetting except for the cover. Because the printer is not required to do the typesetting, you can save hundreds of dollars and cut production time in half through the offset method of book printing. For detailed information on the preparation of pages, refer to the section on "Preparing Pages for Offset Printing."

Offset printing is also ideal for the reprinting of previously printed books.

Preparing Manuscript For Typeset Printing: Your manuscript to be submitted to the printer for typeset printing should be neatly typed, double spaced, on one side of 8½x11 white bond typewriter paper, with a minimum number of changes or corrections marked. If there are many changes on the page, retype it. Remember that the first page of the book is the title page, and the second page (back of the title page) is the copyright page. Number your pages, check spelling, punctuation and grammar. Indicate where pictures, charts and photographs are to go.

Your best friend will be your dictionary. One of the best is *Webster's Ninth New Collegiate Dictionary* ($15.95). The best is *Webster's Third New International Dictionary* ($79.95). The printer is apt to reject poorly prepared copy. Most will not accept handwritten manuscripts. Many typists specialize in the preparation of manuscripts to be submitted to printers. You will find them advertising in the pages of *Writer's Digest* or *The Writer* magazines. Charges for typing range from $1.00 to $2.00 per page, and include minor corrections and one carbon copy. Keep a copy of your original manuscript. There have been cases of manuscripts lost or damaged in the mails, or destroyed by fire in the printing plant.

Request proofs from your printer if he is to do the typesetting. This will enable you to see how your copy will look when typeset, and to correct any typesetting errors that may have occurred in the course of setting your manuscript in type. You can also make changes from original copy, but these are known as "Author's Alterations" and you will be charged by your printer on a time basis. If you expect to make extensive changes or corrections, ask the printer to send a set of galley proofs before the page proofs. You will be able to proofread your copy before it is made up into pages. When page proofs are submitted, any major changes that require rearranging of material on each page is an expensive operation, and the printer will require the author to pay for this additional work.

Proofs should be carefully read, either by yourself or better yet, by another person, and corrections plainly marked in the margin, preferably in ink or colored pencil. The printer is not responsible for errors not corrected on the proofs. Book proofs carry regular third or fourth class postage and are not entitled to the Special Rate applicable to books or manuscripts.

No matter how carefully you proofread the pages, some errors may escape your attention. Don't be too concerned as errors are found even in the best selling books. If it is a minor typographical error, such as transposition of letters in a word, make a note to correct in a future reprint. If it is a serious error such as a date, a name or a material fact, print an "erratum" slip indicating the corrections, and insert one such slip in the front of each book. This procedure is also recommended when it becomes necessary to update material in the book.

For additional information about the rules of manuscript preparation, with specific data on typing, grammar, punctuation, indexing, proofreading, and authors' rights, purchase a copy of *Preparing Your Manuscript*, available for $8.95 from The Writer, Inc., 120 Boylston St., Boston, MA 02116.

Preparing Pages for Offset Printing: If you are an accurate typist, you should have no problem preparing "camera ready" pages for offset printing. The average typist can prepare an attractive and legible page that will be sharp and clear. For best results, use a good typewriter with clean type and fresh ribbon. Use correction tape or correction fluid to type over errors. The paper should be good quality bond typewriter paper. Do not use "erasable" paper.

To make your page look most like regular printed type, we recommend an electric typewriter with carbon ribbon. One of the best machines is the IBM Selectric II or III with lift-off correction tape. It is simple to operate and has interchangeable elements that permits you to choose your preferred type face. If you are not in a position to buy, you can rent a machine from a typewriter agency. If you feel that you cannot do justice to the typing, get it done by a professional typist. A number of typists advertise in *Writer's Digest* and *The Writer*. Or better yet, ask your printer to recommend an experienced typist.

The title page is the first page; the copyright page is the next page. A page is one side of the "sheet"; the page on the back is another page. We recommend that pages be typed single spaced with double spacing between paragraphs. To improve the eye appeal, you can "justify" the page (make an even right hand margin) by inserting extra spaces between words so that the last letter of each line ends under the last letter of the preceding line. The neater and sharper the typewritten page, the nicer appearing will be the final printed page. And don't forget the page number.

It is important to type each page in the proper area for the size book you anticipate printing. If you prepare your page in too large an area, it will be necessary to reduce your page to the extent that the resulting printed type will be too small to be read. A good idea is to type one representative page and send it to the printer for his approval.

Here are printing areas for typing various size books:

6x9 book—printing area	4¾x7½
for 10% reduction	5¼x8¼
15% reduction	5½x8¾
20% reduction	5¾x9
5½x8½ book—printing area	4¼x7
for 10% reduction	4¾x7¾
15% reduction	5x8½
20% reduction	5¼x8¾
5x7 book—printing area	3¾x5½
for 10% reduction	4-1/8x6
15% reduction	4¼x6¼
20% reduction	4½x6 5/8
4¼x7 book—printing area	3¼x6
for 10% reduction	3½x6½
15% reduction	3¾x7
20% reduction	4x7¼

Refer to the back of this book for samples of pages typed in different areas and reduced to fit a 5½x8½ page. If you plan to use a word processor, it might be well to invest $2.95 for a copy of *An Authors Primer to Word Processing,* available from AAP Higher Education Division, One Park Avenue, N.Y.C., N.Y. 10016.

Artwork and Photographs: There should be no problem in printing illustrations, art work and photographs. If your pages are being prepared for offset, your line drawings should be pasted into position on the pages and there would be no extra charge for printing. If you have shaded art work or photographs, do not paste these on the pages. The printer will screen them, reduce or enlarge them, and strip them into place where you have left a space for printing. In typeset printing, indicate where the illustrations and photographs are to be printed. These also have to be screened and stripped into place.

Identify each illustration or photograph by placing a number in light pencil on the back of the photo. Enter this same number on your offset page or on the manuscript page. The cost of printing shaded illustrations and photographs is always in addition to the printing of the inside pages. The cost remains the same regardless of the number of copies printed.

Many book printers can reproduce your full color photographs and art work on covers, dust jackets and inside pages. This involves making special color separated negatives, which cost approximately $300 to $400 for each photograph or illustration. Contact your printer to determine if he can print in full color.

There are professional art studios that prepare art work for covers or inside pages. You can find artists listed in local telephone books. Or ask your printer to recommend an artist. Perhaps you are talented enough to do the illustrations yourself or have a friend who can help you. Many authors find high school or college art teachers interested in working with them for a reasonable charge.

Another source of art work is the "Clip Art" books that contain drawings and illustrations that you can use without charge once you buy the book. These books come in various categories, such as religious, sports, holidays, animals, flowers, etc. Books sell for about $25 and contain numerous drawings. Contact Clipper Creative Art Service, 6000 N. Forest Park Dr., P.O. Box 1901, Peoria, IL. 61657; or Volk Clip Art, P.O. Box 72, Pleasantville, N.J. 08232; or Cliptips, Mead Paper Marketing Communications, Courthouse Plaza NE, Dayton, OH 45463.

Pseudonyms and Company Names: If, for some reason, you prefer not to use your name as author of your book, you can adopt a pseudonym, also known as a pen name. There is no legal problem involved. You can still secure a copyright under this name although you will have to reveal your true name on the copyright application.

To add prestige to your book, it might be a good idea to use a publisher's company name on the cover and title page. Establish a business name for yourself such as "Smith Press," "Jones Publishing Co.," "Brown Publishers," or similar. Check with your local County Clerk if this name has to be registered. If you do not wish to reveal your home address, rent a postoffice box as a mail address for receipt of orders and correspondence. Cost for boxes is low. Perhaps your printer will allow you to use his logo, and his publisher's name and address in your book.

Paper and Cover Stocks: Most paperback books are printed on 50# white book or offset paper, and bound in a glossy kromekote cover. Hard bound books and books with many photographs or illustrations should use the heavier 60# or 70# paper. Where thickness is preferred, the 70# vellum paper will do the job. Of course, the heavier the paper, the more the printing will cost.

Paperback books of less than 72 inside pages are usually "saddle stitched" with two staples in the center of the book. Books that contain 72 or more pages are "perfect bound" with adhesives to make a square back book. The advantage of square back books is that the title and author's name can be printed on the side (spine). Book pages bound in hard covers are Smyth sewn with thread.

Quality B cloth is generally used on hard covered books. If your hard covered book will be displayed in bookstores, it is well to order protective dust jackets. While these jackets are printed on almost all qualities of paper, 80# white or colored enamel stock seems to be the preferred choice. If tastefully printed and illustrated, a dust jacket will enhance the appearance and sales appeal of any book. To keep books clean and fresh looking, have each book wrapped in a transparent plastic bag, known as "shrink wrapping."

Other types of bindings are also available. Plastic spiral binding is ideal for recipe books or workbooks that need to lay perfectly flat when open. Another type is loose leaf binding, enabling pages to be removed and replaced with new pages.

How Many Books Shall I Order? It is a good point to remember that the major cost of setting up your typeset book is the initial typesetting. The most economical quantity to order is 1,000. In quantities of less than 1,000, the cost per book is materially increased. For example, if you are ordering a 200 page 5½x8½ typeset book, paperback covers, the cost for 250 copies would be about $11.44 per book. If 1,000 copies were ordered, the cost would be reduced to $3.95 per book. Of course, if there is no possibility of selling or distributing more than 250 copies, it would be considered false economy to order 1,000 copies just for the sake of reducing the cost per book.

What About Future Reprints? Once the book has been printed, whether typeset or offset, additional printings can be reproduced by offset at less cost than for the original printing. Most printers save the offset negatives for several years for future reprints. Reprints will reproduce as well as the initial printing, and it is even possible to make minor additions and corrections.

How Much Shall I Charge for My Book? Ordinarily, a good theory is to charge three or four times the cost of production. A book costing the author $3 each to produce should be sold for $8.95 to $10.95. This will take care of advertising and other promotion costs, and will leave a fair profit for the author or seller. Where books are to be sold through distributors or bookstores, the selling price of the book should be four to five times the cost of production. Bookstores are allowed a 40% discount from list, while wholesale distributors receive 5% additional. Libraries are given a 25% discount. It is important to keep your selling price down to a point where it is competitive with the price of other books of similar content and size. Otherwise, you may price your book out of the market. If your book has a large sales potential, the cost of production can be reduced by increasing your print order to 2,000 or even 5,000 copies. No book can be profitably sold for less than six dollars, regardless of production cost to the author. Do not compare your book to the $4.95 to $6.95 paperbacks sold by the hundreds of thousands in book stalls. These books are printed in from 100,000 to 500,000 quantities.

Everyone likes a bargain. It is good psychology to print a price on the book in excess of what the author expects to get for his book. Thus an ad reading "Published to sell for $7 – available direct from the author for a limited time only for $5.95" will pull better than a similar ad offering the book for sale at $5.95. Note that it is better to charge $5.95 instead of $6.00, $6.95 instead of $7.00. Psychology of selling again. Price of the book should be printed on front cover.

It is important to determine if your state law requires a sales tax on either local or out-of-state book sales.

Bookstores are notoriously slow in paying their bills. Some never pay at all and others may pay after several billings. Some require billing in triplicate or quadruplicate, making it most difficult for the small self-publishing author-distributor. We recommend that you require payment in full with order by printing a small circular: "Due to the high cost of bookkeeping and billing on small orders, we now require payment in full with order." Always require customer to pay the postage charges. Stay away from sending orders C.O.D.

and make sure that you have payment in advance when making shipments to customers in foreign countries.

Choosing Your Printer: While there are a number of fine book printing firms in all parts of the country, many of them are too large for the average author. They may be interested only in minimum quantities of 5,000 or more. Because they are located in high cost labor areas or in expensive rental districts, printing prices may be high. On the other hand, smaller printers do not have the equipment or know-how to produce books of high quality. The problem then is to find a suitable printing house to produce a good job at lowest possible cost.

The Adams Press, 30 W. Washington Street, Chicago, Illinois 60602, has been producing books for over forty-five years, both typeset and offset. They cater to the author who has a limited publishing budget. They can handle any size book, from 48 to 1,000 pages, and in lots of 250 copies up, both in paperback and cloth bound editions. Because they specialize in a limited number of paper and cover stocks, and operate under a unique payment plan, prices are generally much lower than those charged by other book printing houses. They offer a free catalog and simplified mail order price list that enables the author to determine the exact cost of his job before placing the order. Workmanship is excellent. A most impressive testimonial is the large list of customers who have had third, fourth and even fifth books printed by them. Adams Press handled the production of the book you are now reading.

Submitting Your Material to the Printer: Now that you have decided to get your book printed, and have determined the size of the page, the type of paper and cover wanted, the approximate number of pages and the number of copies you will need, you are ready to submit the material and order to the printer. In most cases, no legal contract is necessary. Both you and the printer have agreed as to the cost of the job, which should be in writing to avoid any future disputes. Be sure that you understand the terms under which you are expected to pay for the printing. Determine how long it will take your printer to complete your job. Not only is this based on the size of the book but on the production schedule of the printer. Good printers operate busy plants. Allow plenty of time to produce your book. Some printers may be able to get the job completed in two or three months while others may require seven or eight months or even longer. Your printer should be able to give an approximate completion date.

Send the material flat in an envelope or box that will withstand rough handling in the mails. If there are to be special arrangements for copy or pictures, submit a "dummy" showing how copy is to be made up and the position of the pictures. Drawings and photographs should be submitted flat with a corrugated backing to prevent folding in the mails. Special photograph mailing envelopes can be purchased in stationery stores. Never paste pictures to copy or "dummy." This might tend to delay your order and some of the pictures might be damaged in removing them from the pages.

Manuscripts can be sent through the mails under a special low rate of postage. Place the endorsement "Special Fourth Class Rate — Contents: Manuscript" on the face of the envelope or package. This will enable you to send your manuscript to any point in the United States at a special rate. For faster delivery, endorse the package "Special Handling." For still faster delivery, send your package by "Priority Mail" or the more expensive "Express Mail." If you would like a receipt from the postoffice showing when the package was received by the printer, add "Certified Mail — Return Receipt Requested."

United Parcel Service also offers a fast and safe method for shipping your package to the printer.

Planning Storage Space: Before the shipment of books arrives, determine where the books will be kept. Store them in a cool dry place. Heat and dampness will tend to yellow the paper or rust the staples used in binding. Excessive moisture will cause the pages of the book to curl. Keep them dust free by leaving them in the original shipping cartons, opening only one carton at a time as the books are needed.

HOW TO SECURE A COPYRIGHT

A copyright protects the material in your book from being reprinted by another person without your written permission. It also adds to the prestige of the book as the author thinks enough about the contents to protect it from unauthorized use. Both published books and unpublished manuscripts are eligible for copyright.

It is a simple matter to secure a copyright, and most authors should have no difficulty in completing the application. To secure the required form, write to the Register of Copyrights, Library of Congress, Washington, D.C. 20559, requesting **Form TX**. This form is used for books published in the United States and Canada, and consists of a two sided 8½x11 sheet with questions about your book and the author.

Progressive book printers will secure the copyright without charge. The copyright exists for the life of the author plus 50 additional years.

It is important that the proper copyright notice be printed on either the title page or verso (back of the title page). The copyright notice must contain three elements: the word copyright (or copr.), the year of publication, and the name of the copyright owner. For example:

Copyright © 1987 by John Doe

The symbol © results in copyright protection in those countries which are members of the Universal Copyright Convention.

Send two copies of the book, the completed and signed application form, and fee of $10 in the same envelope to the copyright office. The length of time it takes the copyright office to process an application and return the copyright certificate varies from time to time, depending on the volume of applications received and the number of personnel available.

The original copyright law went into effect in 1790 with a major revision in 1978. The copyright office receives more than 155,000 applications annually, not only covering books but also phonorecords. For additional information about the copyright laws, write for **Circular R1, Copyright Basics**.

HOW TO FILE FOR A
LIBRARY OF CONGRESS CATALOG CARD NUMBER

Filing for a Preassigned Number: The Library of Congress prepares a Catalog Card for each book called to its attention and sends printed copies of these cards to over 19,000 libraries that subscribe to Library of Congress Catalog Cards. Some of the larger libraries buy copies of almost every book recorded on these cards. In addition, all books currently acquired and cataloged by the Library of Congress are listed in *The National Union Catalog*, regularly printed in nine monthly issues, three quarterly cumulations, and in annual and quinquennial cumulations. Practically all public and private libraries subscribe to these catalogs.

It is possible to secure a preassigned catalog card number in advance of publication, which can be printed in the book to show that it has been recorded. To secure the necessary form, write to Library of Congress, Cataloging in Publication Division, Washington, D.C. 20540, and ask for "Request for Preassignment of Library of Congress Catalog Card Number." This is a simple one page form with few questions. Complete this form and return to the same address. Within a few days, you will receive a photocopy of the form with the Library of Congress catalog card number entered.

The preassigned number is entered on the copyright page under the copyright notice, using the following legend:

Library of Congress catalog card number 87-12345
(with your own number, of course)

When books are printed, send one copy to the Library. The Library of Congress will send postage free mailing labels for use in sending the completed copy of the book. This copy is used for cataloging purposes in order to print catalog cards which you find in library card files by title of book, author's name, and subject. This copy is in addition to the two copies sent to the copyright office. The plan, as a whole, is deliberately separate from the copyright procedure.

There is no charge for securing a catalog card number. Progressive book printers will handle the details for you at no extra cost. The Library of Congress began issuing card numbers in 1902 and now issues about 17,000 pre-assigned numbers a year.

HOW TO OBTAIN AN
INTERNATIONAL STANDARD BOOK NUMBER

The ISBN system is an internationally accepted system for the numbering of books for ease of title, publisher and edition identification. Each publisher is given a publisher identifier as a prefix number, and then assigned a series of additional numbers. The publisher assigns one of these numbers to each of the titles that he issues.

The ISBN is printed on the reverse of the title page under the copyright notice and the Library of Congress catalog card number, and on the lower right hand corner of the outside back cover or dust jacket. Many publishers include ISBN's in catalogs, and on advertisements and other promotional materials. About 90% of the titles in print in the United States have ISBN's assigned to them.

To secure an ISBN (or a series of numbers for more than one book), request an *Application for ISBN Publishers Prefix* from ISBN U.S. Agency, 205 East 42nd Street, N.Y.C., N.Y. 10017. There is no cost involved.

The number lends an aura of professionalism, and self-publishing authors are urged to apply for it. Numbers are assigned only to publishers and not to printers. File early and enter the number in the proper places in the manuscript before sending order to the printer.

Nothing dresses up your book more than an attractive art designed cover. Here are a few samples:

by DON ARMANDO

How to Promote Your Book

Pre-publication Announcements: Even while your book is in the process of being printed, it might be well to send out pre-publication notices announcing the publication of your book. The circulars should give a description of the book content, price, and where it can be purchased. These can be mailed to prospective purchasers, to friends and relatives of the author, and to home town newspapers and bookstores. It also helps to have a friendly newspaper columnist or radio-television commentator give the book a pre-publication plug. A special pre-publication discount price for the book might stimulate advance sales. Be sure that the anticipated delivery date of your book is not underestimated. It is better to indicate a date of a month or two later than expected to save needless correspondence if there are delays in the completion and receipt of the finished copies.

Free Publicity in Cumulative Book Index: Your book will be listed in *Cumulative Book Index,* published by the H. W. Wilson Company, 950 University Avenue, Bronx, NY 10452, by filling out an Information Slip available upon request. A copy of the book or some descriptive material should accompany the Information Slip.

The *Cumulative Book Index* is published monthly, with cumulations through the year and a final two year cumulation every other year. The index lists all books printed in the English language and is distributed to approximately 10,000 libraries and bookstores.

The best way to insure a listing is to send one copy of your book to *Cumulative Book Index.* This will enable them to record accurately the bibliographical data. They also route the newly received books to other units for possible further listings. By sending a copy of your publication, you have the possibility, therefore, of other listings besides CBI. They do not include books of less than 100 pages or books which are in a printing of fewer than 500 copies. There is no charge for a listing in CBI.

Free Listing in Publishers' Weekly: From a form letter sent out by the Booklisting Department of this publication: "We would like to make sure that we receive your new books regularly for free listing in the Weekly Record of *Publishers' Weekly.* Thus we try to make a complete list of books published in the United States. *Publishers'*

Weekly reaches a subscription list of more than 38,000 book sellers, libraries and other book purchasing markets. The Weekly Record is highly regarded as a checklist and buying guide."

"If you will send us your new books as soon as they are ready, we will enter them, giving bibliographical details and brief descriptions of their contents. We would like to receive copies as far in advance of publication as possible, although we do not list them until the week of publication. To simplify matters we would appreciate your making a notation of the prices and publication dates inside the front cover of all books sent to us."

Send your book to "Weekly Record of *Publishers' Weekly,*" 205 E. 42nd St., N.Y.C., NY 10017. Your book will also be automatically listed in the *American Book Publishing Record.* Subscription price to *Publishers' Weekly* is $84.00 per year.

Free Listings in New York Times: The "Books Published Today" column is a selective listing of books received by the Daily Book Page office of the *New York Times.* It does not include books that are technical or of special interest, nor does it include text books, juveniles, or doctoral theses. If interested in having your book listed, send a copy to "Daily Book Page," *New York Times,* Times Square, N.Y.C., N.Y. 10036.

The *Times* also lists books in the Sunday Book Review Section. This is a separate department from that described in the previous paragraph. Send books to Editor, Sunday Book Review Section, *New York Times,* Times Square, N.Y.C., NY 10036. The *New York Times* has a circulation of 1,702,000.

Free Listing in Small Press Record: The *Small Press Record of Books In Print* is an annual publication that lists 16,000 books published by self-publishing authors and small presses. Each item is indexed by author, title, publisher (with address) and price. Book advertising is also accepted. Available for $29.95 a copy. Send them a copy of your book and descriptive material. Address: Small Press Record, Box 100, Paradise, CA 95969.

This same publisher lists newly published small press books in *Small Press Review,* a monthly publication with a circulation of 3,000. Each issue carries book reviews of recently self-published books. Subscription price is $22.00 per year.

"To Eternity and Back"

by *Laura Ellen Winsor*

THERE IS NO DEATH—There are no barriers—Space is no limitation. There is no time—No past—No future —ONLY—THE—NOW. This is the fundamental message which "To Eternity and Back" proclaims.

My beloved friends; I am not in the least a pessimist. In fact I am by nature an optimist. But we cannot close our eyes and deafen our ears, or turn our minds away from the signs of the times. We are approaching a new era, a new cycle. We need have no doubt about the ultimate outcome. We must know that there is something in the soul of every man that will cause him instinctively to take the side of right and justice. Man is not merely a shell of flesh and blood, but a part of the life force that sustains the Universe. Part of the infinite power that causes the heavens to glow,— the sun to shine and the birds to sing.

We are all children of the same creator, and the same spiritual destiny awaits us all. Let us rejoice that freedom and liberty are before us. That new ideas, ideals, values, aims and authorities will launch each and every one of us upon broader interpretations of life.

Pre-fabricated cover (crushed leather) **PRICE $3.95**

Publication in July, 1960. Special pre-publication offer until date of publication only, $3.50. Each copy of "To Eternity and Back" will be personally autographed by the author if desired. ☐ Yes ☐ No

MAIL YOUR ORDER IN NOW — USE THE HANDY ORDER FORM BELOW

(Sample of a pre-publication announcement)

(Sample of a pre-publication announcement)

Free Listing in Books in Print, Publishers Trade List Annual, and Subject Guide to Books in Print: You can get invaluable free publicity for your book in these three important book guides. These books are published annually and reach thousands of libraries, bookstores, book wholesalers and overseas book buyers.

Books in Print ($199.95) lists over 665,000 in-print books, old and new, from 17,500 U.S. publishers, indexed by author and title.

Publishers Trade List Annual ($124.95) lists books published by 1,800 publishers, big and small.

Subject Guide to Books in Print ($142.95) contains a subject index to almost every U.S. book in print, over 575,000 listings.

Other books by the same publisher are:
American Book Publishing Record ....($199.00)
American Book Trade Directory ....($129.95)
Children's Books in Print.................................($62.95)
Cumulative Paperback Index ....($58.00)
Large Type Books in Print ....($59.00)

To be considered for listing in these book guides, request an "Advance Book Information" form from ABI Department, R.R. Bowker Company, 205 East 42nd St., N.Y.C., NY 10017. There is no charge for these listings. You can probably find copies of these books in your local library.

Other Free Listings: The Library Corporation, P.O. Box 40035, Washington, D.C. 20016, is the publisher of *Any-Book*, listing new books in print which are sent to thousands of bookstores and libraries. Write for listing form. There is no charge.

You can have a free listing in the *American Drop-Shippers Directory* if you are willing to drop ship books. That means that other firms will include your book in their catalogs and sell it at the retail price. They will send you a shipping label addressed to the buyer of your book, together with a remittance for the wholesale price, at which time you will ship the book. Write for a listing questionnaire to World Wide Trade Service, Medina, WA 98039.

Another similar directory is the *Book Dealers Dropship Directory* published by the American Bookdealers Exchange, P.O. Box 2525, La Mesa, CA 92041. They are also publishers of *Book Dealers World*.

Advertising in AB Bookman's Yearbook: This is the specialist book world annual where over 500 publishers advertise their books. Reaches over 7,100 booksellers, dealers, publishers, librarians and collectors. Write *AB Bookman's Yearbook*, Box AB, Clifton, NJ 07015. Printed in two volumes—sells for $15.00 a set. This firm also publishes the *AB Bookman's Weekly*, circulation 8,000, subscription rate: $50.00 per year.

Book Reviews: One of the most effective methods of promoting your book would be to have it reviewed in magazines or newspapers. However, for the first published author, it is difficult to get a book review printed. Most reviewers prefer to report on books by established authors, or by well-known personalities. However, if your book has special appeal, it should be submitted for possible review to publications reaching that particular group. For example, if your book concerns horseracing, it should be sent to the turf journals; if it is about flowers, it should be sent to the gardening magazines; if it treats the subject of writing, it should be submitted to the writers' publications.

A good bet that should not be overlooked is the home town newspaper. If you live in a smaller community, the fact that a local resident has had a book published is first page news. This is more effective publicity than an actual review. As most newspapers cannot spare the time of an individual to read your book for review, you might prepare such a review yourself for submission to the editor.

If you are unable to write an effective review, have it done professionally by Carol Ann Osley, 115 Willis Ave., Herkimer, NY 13350. Write for cost and details.

Autograph Parties: If you can persuade a local bookstore to sponsor an autograph party, and this is advertised in the locality where you are known, you might be able to sell a number of autographed books. However, with unknown authors, book shops may not be interested in going to the bother and expense of an autograph party. If you have unlimited promotion expense, and are willing to underwrite the cost of the newspaper advertising, you may find some shops receptive. They have little to lose and the free advertising of their shop more than offsets any inconvenience of the autograph party. Again, the successful parties are those held by established authors or important personalities in the news.

Advertising in Publications: Advertise wisely and slowly. Your funds can be quickly depleted by unproductive advertising. If the book has limited reader appeal, advertise in publications that reach the potential buyer. If it is a "do-it-yourself" type, consider the many mechanics magazines that reach this reader. If there is a special appeal to women, use the pages of publications read by women.

Books of general appeal, either fiction or non-fiction, can be advertised in the book sections of newspapers and magazines. Many newspapers have book supplements, usually with the Sunday issues. The largest book supplements are:

The New York Times Book Review (Sun.)
229 W. 43rd Street
N.Y.C., NY 10036
(Circulation 1,702,000)

Book World (Sun.)
Washington Post
1150 15th St. N.W.
Washington, D.C. 20071
(Circulation 1,065,782)

The Book Review (Sun.)
Los Angeles Times
Times Mirror Square
Los Angeles, CA 90053
(Circulation 1,347,000)

For advertising rates, write direct to the publishers. If you plan an extensive advertising campaign, secure the services of an advertising agency. There is no extra charge, as the advertising agency receives a commission from the publisher. Avoid big agencies that are not interested in small accounts. Listed below are agencies handling small order accounts. They will send you free rate guides upon request. These guides list advertising rates for magazines and newspapers. Agencies will also prepare your copy and art work on a time charge basis.

Chicago Advertising Agency
28 E. Jackson Blvd.
Chicago, IL 60604

Columbia Advertising Agency
P.O. Box 1285
Richmond, IN 47374

Morlock Advertising Agency
188 W. Randolph Street
Chicago, IL 60601

National Advertising
Box 5
Sarasota, FL 33578

For a complete list of newspapers and magazines that have special book columns, refer to Literary Market Place ($75.00), 205 E. 42nd St., N.Y.C., NY 10017. You can probably examine a copy in your local public library.

The experience of many authors and small publishers has been that the results from advertising most often fail to pay the cost of the ad. For example, the smallest display ad that you can place in *Writer's Digest* is $590 for one insertion. The least expensive ad in *Modern Maturity Magazine* (the publication of the American Association of Retired Persons—circulation 13,000,000) is $25,000 for one insertion.

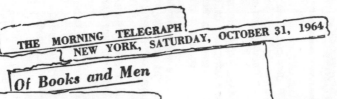

THE MORNING TELEGRAPH
NEW YORK, SATURDAY, OCTOBER 31, 1964

Of Books and Men

Page A14   THE SACRAMENTO BEE
Saturday, February 22, 1964

ON THE BOOKSHELF—
Novel Is Tale About 4th Century Martyrs

CONSTANTINE'S TRI-UMPH, A TALE OF THE ERA OF THE MARTYRS by W. H. Spears, Jr.; Adams Press; $3.95.

Spears' book is a novel about the age of the persecution of Christians under Emperors Diocletian and Galerius.

The hero is a young Greek

W. H. Spears Jr. has told the tale of Constantine, the Roman Emperor of the Fourth Century, who brought Christianity to the Empire in direct contrast to his predecessor, Diocletian, whose persecutions were largely political. Mr. Spears tells the story well in "Constantine's Triumph" (Adams Press, $3.95). In the vast panorama of history his individual characters stand out and are believable.

▼

Helen MacInnes, who has written exciting and literate thrillers ... in classic countries ...

juxtaposes Italian home life, whether Roman or exalted, Sicilian, or bourgeois, with the fashion... teries proliferated in ony. The author has ... e knowledge of film-n... nique as well as of ... iting; his novel is i... as well as ... salvi.

The Windsor Star

Old Rome Recreated

By H. L. M.

W. H. Spears, Jr., has set himself to the considerable task of writing a series of novels based on Gibbon's "Decline and Fall of the Roman Empire." CONSTANTINE'S TRIUMPH: A Tale of the Era of the Martyrs (Adams Press) is the first.

Novel Of Empire Entertaining

CONSTANTINE'S TRI-UMPH, A TALE OF THE ERA OF THE MARTYRS. By J. H. Spears Jr. Adams Prss. 51 pages. $3.95.

BY J. L. ARNOLD
A Review

W. H. Spears Jr.'s first novel about the decline and fall of the Roman Empire would be helpful to history students of that era and to those interested in the persecutions of Christians under the Emperor Diocletian.

The story is woven around

Phrygia to escape persecution. They are captured, and Anacreon is sent to the copper mines. While there, his right eye is cut out and his left heel burned with hot irons. infliction was the badge of a Christian.

Marcia was tried for treason and sentenced to die in the arena where people were fed to wild beasts.

Anacreon was freed from the copper mines by Constantine's army on its march to ... forces with ... he could ... ill Lucius, ... could have ... Marcia and ... ad her life

THE MURRAY HILL NEWS

IN THE HEART OF NEW YORK
"The Richest Section in the World"

Among Our Publishers
By PEGGY HUNTLEY

"Constantine's Triumph," is a tale of the era of Martyrs, written by W. H. Spears, Jr., would appeal to the religious and politically minded. The early centuries are revealed through a Greek scholar and his Roman bride who become followers of Christ, through this novel about the decline and fall of the Roman Empire. It is interesting, sells for $3.95 by [East Ma... Heights.]

stie, writ... Mary W... ntic and... g genius... sical back... ussia an... re and a... iant's Br... o intent... conscious... e succeed...

falls restl... on hi... Rome... and f... Luciu... and... ploys... secre... Em... ning... move... that... being... reno...

THE BOOK EXCHANGE

CONSTANTINE'S TRIUMPH. A Tale of the Era of the Martyrs. By W. H. Spears, Jr. (The Author, 304 East Marion Avenue, Prospect Heights, Illinois, U.S.A. 9 by 6 ins. 262 pp. Cl. D.w. $3.95.) The first in an intended series of novels about the decline and fall of the Roman Empire, this book tells the story of a young Grecian scholar who travels to Rome to complete his studies, where he falls in love with a patrician girl who has secret sympathy for the early Christian church. Later he meets Constantine, the young Roman tribune destined to be the first Christian Emperor. The story is well told,

"CONSTANTINE'S TRI-UMPH", a tale of the era of the myrtyrs by W. H. Spears, Jr. The first of a series of novels on the fall of the Roman Empire in modern language for moderns. (Adams, 30 W. Washington, Chicago, $3.95.)

dissed the major old Lamb wrote ntine was of estry. On the y of French enri Daniel-Rops, St. Helena.

behalf. It seems

W. H. Spears, Jr.
304 East Marion Avenue
Prospect Heights, Illinois

(Sample Book Reviews)

Neat little book stuffed with treasures of Depression

Close to home

"HOBNAIL BOOTS AND KHAKI SUITS"

By E. Kay Kiefer and Paul E. Fellows
Adams Press; $14.95 hardcover,
$9.95 paperback

Reviewed by MARY SCARPINATO

A brief look at the Great Depression and the Civilian Conservation Corps as seen through the eyes of those who were there" is the way E. Kay Kiefer and Paul E. Fellows describe their book. The authors, both residents of Southern Illinois, have drawn much material from local interviews.

And their study is a refreshing look at another American era in this golden anniversary year of the CCC's founding as-a federal environmental work corps for the nation's unemployed. (The CCC was disbanded near the time of the U.S.'s entry into World War II.)

The pleasure of this book comes from history honed into easy reading matter, often arranged in alternately humorous and poignant vignettes.

Browsing its pages is like finding some forgotten trunk in the attic stuffed with such treasures as old photographs, yellow newspaper clippings and youthful diaries.

In fact, all these have been culled and then fit into neat style along with recent interviews of former CCC members.

Here are some examples:

From a young Illinois recruit's diary:

June 20 — Was on M.P. duty on the beach and had a good time with a drunkard who pulled a fish out of his pocket and wanted me to hear it tick.

June 23 — Everything was going fine this morning when all of the sudden they called and told us to get our tents prepared because the "Secretary of War" was coming to visit the camp. We were all lined up slick and trim at the appointed time. . . . We waited for two hours and finally "he" arrived. All he did was ride up one street and down another where no one could see him.

Aug. 13 — I had a good time K.P.ing and I got six ice cream cups and everything else I wanted to eat.

From a recruit's recollection of his father:

It wasn't long before he was laid off due to the Depression, and he never had another job the rest of his life. . . . My father was a religious man. He didn't smoke, drink or use rough language. He felt it was his job to support his family and he couldn't do it. I guess he just couldn't take it anymore. One day he just put on his hat and walked out the back door and never came home. They shipped his body back from Tucson 25 years later.

Mary Scarpinato is a Globe-Democrat staff writer.

Midwestern CCC recruits are shown in training at Fort Sheridan in 1933.

(Sample Book Review)

(Samples of Book Ads)

(Sample of a Book Ad)

Enregistré à New York,
cet hebdomadaire est édité par
Joseph & Joseph Publishers

Haïti-Observateur
50 Court Street
Brooklyn, N.Y. 11201
Tél. (718) 834-0222

New York: 50¢

Hors de New York: 60¢
Régions à plus de 100 miles: 75¢
Montréal, Miami, Boston,
Washington: 75¢

4-11 avril 1986

Lè manke gid, pèp la gaye

HAÏTI OBSERVATEUR

VOL. XVI No. 14

Un excellent ouvrage de Eva Pataki

« HAITIAN PAINTINGS, Art and Kitsch »

Le livre que Eva Pataki vient de faire paraître représente l'une des plus importantes contributions à l'histoire de la culture haïtienne, et particulièrement à l'un de ses aspects les plus originaux: la peinture.

La bibliographie sur l'art et la peinture en Haïti n'est pas très riche et l'on peut compter sur les doigts les ouvrages qui ont été écrits sur la peinture haïtienne, son histoire et ses peintres.

Certes, « Haïti et ses peintres », de Michel Philippe Lerebours est un livre capital et sert toujours de référence à ceux qui veulent explorer le champ de la peinture en Haïti.

Mais « Haitian Painting » de Eva pataki vient à son heure, à un moment où la peinture haïtienne connaît ses plus beaux moments et est regardée par les connaisseurs et les critiques, même au niveau international, comme une de ces peintures d'avant-garde, dont l'originalité et le primitivisme sont l'un de ses plus beaux fleurons.

Eva Pataki, née en Roumanie de parents hongrois, est tombée amoureuse de la peinture haïtienne, à la suite d'une visite en Haïti. Elle devait en revenir bouleversée. Puis, elle retourna dans ce « paradis » pour s'imprégner, s'enliser dans cette culture.

Aujourd'hui, elle nous offre cet « Haitian Painting » qui est un excellent ouvrage, écrit par un spécialiste ayant fait de solides études en art, à St. Johns University, à Queens College, Columbia University, (Teachers College).

« Haitian Painting » est un ouvrage admirable, rédigé par un vrai connaisseur. Ecrit dans la langue de Shakespeare, il sera lu, commenté par des millions de lecteurs et tous ceux-là pour qui le « primitivisme » haïtien en peinture représente l'une des grandes révolutions dans l'histoire de l'art en général.

Joe Thévenin

(Sample Book Review)

SOMERTON PRESS
PUBLISHERS OF SOCIALLY RELEVANT BOOKS
P.O. BOX 1746   SOMERTON, ARIZONA 85350   (602)627-8140

ANNOUNCES: { **INSIGHT** AND **UNDERSTANDING NOW:**
The Publication of an Important and Unique Study of an American Maximum Security Prison—in crisis. A candid look, inside/outside/top/bottom—

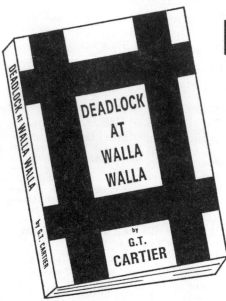

DEADLOCK AT WALLA WALLA

by

G. T. CARTIER

DEADLOCK AT WALLA WALLA
is a top to bottom, cross-sectional documentary study of the Washington State Penitentiary at Walla Walla, Washington.

DEADLOCK AT WALLA WALLA
covers the issues, the proposed solutions, the multitude of details, the individuals, the agony of prison life today.

DEADLOCK AT WALLA WALLA
is descriptive not prescriptive. It's purpose is to share an understanding of all the interlocking elements of American prisons and prison life just as it occurred over a one year period at Walla Walla.

DEADLOCK AT WALLA WALLA
presents the facts and commentaries in a chronological, but kaleidoscopic fashion. Gradually, the characters and themes coalesce into a full, multi-faceted, factual study of prison life at Walla Walla.

FACT #1—Prisons in America today represent our society's most explosive problem. The expanding prison population shows no sign of slowing. Strains on Federal and State Corrections budgets are at the breaking point.

FACT #2— This seemingly unsolvable social problem, in reality, vitally affects all citizens—the taxpayers, the prisoners, ex-prisoners, all of us—and yet no answers are forthcoming—from anyone.

FACT #3— If an answer is to be found, it must begin with insight and understanding of the problem itself. This is the reason *DEADLOCK AT WALLA WALLA* is must reading for all citizens of America today.

1986, 327 pages, ISBN 0-934129-00-2, LC 85-91524

(Book Announcement with Order Blank on Back)

Advertising Direct by Mail: Another method of advertising is to contact potential buyers direct by mail. This can be accomplished by printing descriptive material about your book and sending it through the mails to prospects, who are expected to fill out an order blank and return it with a remittance for a copy of your book.

Purchase a mailing list through any advertising agency (about $55 per thousand names). If your book appeals to a specialized group, you can buy names of doctors, lawyers, teachers, mothers, senior citizens, home owners, etc. A list of over 700,000 buyers of books is available on labels from F & W Publishing, 9933 Alliance Rd., Cincinnati, OH 45242. Another source for names of book buyers is Ahrend Associates, Inc., 800 Fifth Avenue, N.Y.C., NY 10011.

You may want to direct your campaign to bookstores or libraries. Purchase names imprinted directly on your #10 envelopes (saves you cost of addressing). These are available from R. R. Bowker Co., 205 E. 42nd St., N.Y.C., NY 10017. They have lists of 24,000 book outlets in the U.S., 12,500 paperback bookstores, 33,500 public libraries in the U.S., and many other lists. Write to Bowker for a complete catalog of available lists.

If you have the time and patience to do your own addressing, purchase the *American Book Trade Directory* ($129.95) listing more than 25,000 booksellers and 1,000 wholesalers in the U.S. and Canada. Also available is the *American Library Directory* ($119.95) listing over 34,000 libraries in the U.S. and Canada. Both directories are available from R. R. Bowker. Lists of school teachers and principals can be purchased from Educational Lists Co., 161 Glen Head Rd., Glen Head, NY 11545.

Direct by mail advertising can be made more profitable by sending out material relating to a number of books, either in catalog form or on separate circulars. The cost of envelopes, postage, and mailing lists remains the same and returns are bound to be higher.

Business Books Marketing Group, P.O. Box 6870, Torrence, CA 90504, offers a cooperative marketing plan for books relating to business.

Direct Mail Promotions, Inc., 342 Madison Ave., N.Y.C., NY 10017, invites small publishers to join their cooperative mailing to public, school and university libraries.

Peggy Glenn, 1106 Main St., Suite 200, Huntington Beach, CA. 92648, has a cooperative package that is mailed to over 4,000 bookstores every six weeks.

PMA, 241 Pacific Coast Highway, Suite 206, Hermosa Beach, CA 90254, mails notices of new books to libraries every three months.

Testimonials: There is no better advertisement than a testimonial from a satisfied reader. Use these in your advertising – you'll find them effective in stimulating sales. Here are examples of letters received from buyers of the booklet you are now reading and from favorable publication reviews:

> "Your valuable little book is just too valuable to keep. Other people keep borrowing it, so it does not do us any good to own it because it is never where it belongs. Enclosed is a check for another copy, which we will hide and keep secret. We have never seen another book like this one, so much good practical information under one cover." – Mrs. S. H. H., Maryland.

> "May I give the author of this little volume a most enthusiastic pat on the back for a job well done! There is so much Mumbo Jumbo about the relationship between an author and his public that I am delighted to see how thoroughly and briefly you have presented information." – P. A. L., Penna.

> "I enjoyed reading your book as it answers all my questions and more. I got more out of it than from the four or five books which cost me a total of more than $25. After reading all those so called advice books there were still many unanswered questions. Your book had all the answers." – B. H. R., New Jersey.

> The *Library Journal* says: "Adams Press, which has printed many books for authors, now has available a useful booklet called 'How to . . . '" The *Book Exchange* (London, England) wrote: "it is a useful manual for the author proposing to publish his own work."

The book review below, which appeared in Publisher's Weekly, resulted in over 200 retail orders and numerous orders and inquiries from book stores and book distributors.

A lot of useful information for the author who doesn't have a regular publisher is contained in a paperback, "How to Publish, Promote and Sell Your Book" by Joseph V. Goodman (*Adams Press,* 30 W. Washington, St., Chicago, IL 60602). The book is revised and it tells how to arrange for printing one's book economically, how to secure copyright, how to do promotion, how to get distribution, Listing in *CBI,* N.Y. *Times, AB* and *PW* Weekly Record and on LC cards is explained; sales and ads by mail are described; concise lists are given of major review media, wholesale and shipping services and – a very practical point – remainder houses. Among much other information are clearcut warnings about "vanity" publishing operations, including Federal Trade Commission orders issued against such companies. Specimens are shown of various forms of typesetting—IBM and other typewriter composition, along with pages set in some typical faces.

Publishers' Weekly

List of Book Reviewers, Book Catalogs and Publications: It is almost impossible to send copies of your book to all the leading book reviewers or publishers of book catalogs, lists and publications in the hope that your book will be reviewed, mentioned, or listed. However, you can send a pre-publication announcement or book review with the notation: "Review Copies Available Upon Request." Those interested in reviewing your book will write for copies. Send literature to:

AB Bookman's Weekly
Box AB
Clifton, NJ 07015

ALA Bulletin
50 E. Huron Street
Chicago, IL 60611

All-Media Services
13415 Ventura Blvd.
Sherman Oaks, CA 91423

American Book Collector
274 Madison Av.
N.Y.C., NY 10016

American Book Publishing Record
205 E.42nd Street
N.Y.C., NY 10017

American Book Review
Box 188, Cooper Station
N.Y.C., NY 10003

American Bookseller
122 E. 42nd St.—Rm. 141
N.Y.C., NY 10168

American Classical Reviews
City University of New York
Queens College
Flushing, NY 11367

American Literature
Duke University Press
College Station, Box 6667
Durham, NC 27708

American Reference Book Annual
Libraries Unlimited
P.O. Box 263
Littleton, CO 80120

AP Newsfeatures
50 Rockefeller Plaza
N.Y.C., NY 10020

Assn. of College Libraries
100 Riverview Center
Middletown, CT 06457

The Baker & Taylor Co.
Book Selection Dept.
50 Kirby Avenue
Somerville, NJ 08876

Gary Baranik
Author & Books
1272 Prospect Avenue
Brooklyn, NY 11218

John Barkham Reviews
27 E. 65th Street
N.Y.C., NY 10021

Marion Benasutti
885 N. Easton, Road, #6A3
Glenside, PA 19038

Best-In Books
205 Moonshadow Court
Rosswell, GA 30075

Best Sellers
Univ. of Scranton Library
Scranton, PA 18510

The Bloomsbury Review
Owaissa Publishing Co.
Box 8928
Denver, CO 80201

Bookaline Co., Inc.
303 W. 10th Street
N.Y.C., NY 10014

Bookletter
2 Park Avenue
N.Y.C., NY 10016

The Booklist
50 E. Huron Street
Chicago, IL 60611

Book Lover
151 W. 75th St.
N.Y.C., NY 10023

Book People, Inc.
2940 Seventh Street
Berkeley, CA 94710

Book Review Digest
950 University Avenue
Bronx, NY 10452

The Book Report
Box 14466
2950 N. High St.
Columbus, OH 43214

Books
75 E. 55th Street
N.Y.C., NY 10022

Books'n Stuff
Book Review Editor
1065 Farmington Lane NE
Atlanta, GA 30319

Booksellers Catalog Service
29 S. Wabash Avenue
Chicago, IL 60603

Bookstore Journal
Box 200, 2620 Venetial Blvd.
Colorado Springs, CO 80901

Bookswest Magazine
2073 Outpost Dr.
Hollywood, CA 90068

Boston Phoenix
Book Review Editor
100 Massachusetts Av.
Boston, MA 02115

Millicent Braverman
1517 Schuyer Rd., Suite A
Beverly Hills, CA 90210

Buckley-Little Book
   Catalog Co.
Box 512—Canal St. Sta.
N.Y.C., NY 10013

Chicago Sun Times
Book Week
401 N. Wabash Avenue
Chicago, IL 60611

Chicago Tribune
Book Review Editor
435 N. Michigan Avenue
Chicago, IL 60611

Choice
Book Review Editor
100 Riverview Center
Middletown, CT 06457

Christian Bookseller
Gunderson Drive &
   Schmale Road
Wheaton, IL 60187

Christian Science Monitor
Monthly Book Review
One Norway Street
Boston, MA 02115

Chronical of Higher Education
1255 23rd Street N.W.
Washington, D.C. 20037

Conch Review of Books
Symphony Circle
102 Normal Avenue
Buffalo, NY 14213

Conference Board Library Bulletin
845 Third Avenue
N.Y.C., NY 10022

Consumers Savers of America
P.O. Box 328
Uncasville, CT 06382

Cowles Syndicate Inc.
715 Locust Street
Des Moines, IA 50304

Velma S. Daniels
1624 Lake Mirror Drive, NW
Winter Haven, FL 33881

Marc Drogin
74 Court Street
Exeter, NH 03833

ERC Reviews
1107 Lexington Avenue
Dayton, OH 45407

Feature News Service
2330 S. Brentwood Blvd.
St. Louis, MO 63144

Forthcoming Books
205 E. 42nd Street
N.Y.C., NY 10017

Fresh Weekly Review
320 S.W. Stack Street, #315
Portland, OR 97204

Burton Frye
P.O. Box 2505
Myrtle Beach, SC 29577

Good Reading
McCosh 22, Princeton Univ.
Princeton, NJ 08540

James E. Hastings
P.O. Box 262
Seward, NE 68434

Alexia Hayes
34 Hume Street
Medford, MA 02155

Richard Heller
Gannett Westchester
90 Daisy Farms Drive
New Rochelle, NY 10804

Rochelle Holt
1719 – 13th Avenue South
Birmingham, AL 35205

Independent News Alliance
255 W. 84th Street
N.Y.C., NY 10024

Interlude Productions
Box 40
Maplewood, NJ 07040

King Features Syndicate
235 E. 45th Street
N.Y.C., NY 10017

Kirkus Reviews
200 Park Avenue South
N.Y.C., NY 10003

Kliath Paperback Book Guide
Watertown Street
Newton, MA 02158

Charles Lee
Presidential Apts., D-1203
Philadelphia, PA 19131

Library Journal
The Book Review
205 E. 42nd St.,
N.Y.C., NY 10017

The Literary Lantern
418 Whitehead Circle
Chapel Hill, NC 27514

The Literary Review
Rutherford, NJ 07070

Los Angeles Herald Examiner
Book Review Editor
Box 2416 – Terminal Annex
Los Angeles, CA 90054

Los Angeles Review of Books
1005 Pruitt Drive
Redondo Beach, CA 90278

Los Angeles Times Syndicate
Book Review Editor
Times Mirror Square
Los Angeles, CA 90053

Daniel Lusk
326 E. Spruce Street
Missoula, MT 59801

Jerry Mack Book Reviews
Box 5200
San Angelo, TX 76902

Mid-Continent Feature Syndicate
Box 1662
Pittsburgh, PA 15230

The Moretus Press, Inc.
P.O. Box 867
Ossining, NY 10562

Miss Beatrice M. Murphy
117 "R" Street, NE
Washington, D.C. 20002

Nat'l Catholic News Service
1312 Massachusetts Avenue NW
Washington, D.C. 20005

National Weekly Edition
The Washington Post
1150 - 15th Street NW
Washington, D.C. 20071

New Age Book Review
Box 324 – Murray Hill Station
N.Y.C., NY 10156

New Boston Review
10B Mt. Auburn Street
Cambridge, MA 02138

News and Reviews of
   The Small Press
Weeks Mills
New Sharon, ME 04955

Newsletter
P.O. Box 703
San Francisco, CA 94101

New Pages
Box 438
Grand Blanc, MI 48439

New York Post
Book Review Editor
210 South Street
N.Y.C., NY 10002

N.Y. Times Book Review
229 W. 43rd Street
N.Y.C., NY 10036

New York Review of Books
250 W. 57th Street
N.Y.C., NY 10107

Openers
American Library Assn.
50 E. Huron Street
Chicago, IL 60611

Pacific Coast Press Bureau
15581 Product Lane
Huntington Beach, CA 92649

Paperback Books in Print
205 E. 42nd Street
N.Y.C., NY 10017

Paperback Catalog Service
Roaring Brook Lake
Putnam Valley, NY 10579

Patrician Productions
145 W. 58th Street
N.Y.C., NY 10019

Paulus Feature Syndicate
Box 1662
Pittsburgh, PA 15230

Win Pendleton
Box 2121
Windermere, FL 32786

Press Pacifica
P.O. Box 47
Kailua, HI 96734

Provident Book Finder
616 Walnut Avenue
Scottdale, PA 15683

Publishers Weekly
205 E. 42nd Street
N.Y.C., NY 10017

Reference Book Review
Box 190954
Dallas, TX 75219

Register and Tribune
  Syndicate
Book Review
715 Locust Street
Des Moines, IA 50304

Rutward
Box 471
Georgetown, CT 06829

San Diego Evening Tribune
Book Review Editor
P.O. Box 191
San Diego, CA 92112

San Francisco Chronical
Book Review Supplement
901 Mission Street
San Francisco, CA 94119

San Francisco Review of Books
Book Review Editor
Box 33-0090
San Francisco, CA 94133

Carl Schleier Reviews
646 Jones Rd.
Rivervale, NJ 07675

School Library Journal
The Book Review
205 E. 42nd Street
N.Y.C., NY 10017

Lloyd Shearer
140 N. Hamilton Drive
Beverly Hills, CA 90211

Small Press Book Review
11 Ferry Lane West
Westport, CT 06880

Small Press Book Review
P.O. Box 176
Southport, CT 06490

Small Press Review
Box 100
Paradise, CA 95969

So. Hamilton Record News
Cynthia A. Rininger
Jewell, IA 50130

Phil Stitt
1740 W. Devonshire
Phoenix, AZ 85015

Tribune Tower
Book Review
435 N. Michigan Avenue
Chicago, IL 60611

George H. Tweney
16600 Marine View Drive SW
Seattle, WA 98166

United Feature Syndicate
200 Park Avenue
N.Y.C., NY 10166

United Press International
1400 "I" Street NW
Washington, D.C. 20005

Univ. of Saskatchewan
Book Review Section
Box 360 Sub. P.O. Box 6
Saskatoon CANADA S7N OWO

Arejas Vakausas
309 Varick Street
Jersey City, NJ 07302

Voice Literary Supplement
The Village Voice
842 Broadway
N.Y.C., NY 10013

West Coast Review of Books
6331 Hollywood Blvd., Suite 1002
Los Angeles, CA 90028

Wilson Library Bulletin
950 University Avenue
Bronx, NY 10452

Women's Review of Books
Wellesley Center
Wellesley, MA 02181

World Wide News Bureau
309 Varick Street
Jersey City, NJ 07302

World Wide Trade Service
Medina, WA 98039

Wholesale Book Distributors: Bookstores and libraries prefer to buy through wholesalers. With thousands of books available, the wholesalers can afford to be selective as to the books they will handle. Send a printed description of your book. The wholesalers normally buy in larger quantities than individual bookstores or libraries.

Baker & Taylor Co.
11 W. 42nd St.
N.Y.C., NY 10036

The Book House, Inc.
208 W. Chicago St.
Jonesville, MI 49250

Book Jobbers Hawaii
287-J Kalihi St.
Honolulu, HI 76819

Bookazine Co., Inc.
303 W. 10th St.
N.Y.C., NY 10014

Bookmen, Inc.
525 N. Third St.
Minneapolis, MN 55401

Campbell and Hall
1075 Commonwealth Av.
Boston, MA 02215

Caroline House
5 S. Frontenac Rd.
Naperville, IL 60540

Dimondstein Book Express
500 Arch Street
Williamsport, PA 17705

Ingram Book Co.
Box 17266 – 347 Reedwood
Nashville, TN 37217

The following distributors may be more receptive
to self-published books

Associated Booksellers
Box 6361 – 147 Mckinley
Bridgeport, CT 06606

Banner World Distribution
13415 Ventura Blvd.
Sherman Oaks, CA 91423

Book Carrier
19534 Club House Rd.
Gaithersburg, MO 20879

Bookpeople, Inc.
2929 Fifth Av.
Berkeley, CA 94710

Bookslinger
213 E. Fourth St.
St. Paul, MN 55101

The Distributors
702 S. Michigan
South Bend, IN 46618

Dugan & Co.
3 Arlyne Dr.
Somerville, NJ 08876

Independent Publishers Group
One Pleasant Av.
Port Washington, NY 11050

Inland Book Distributors
22 Hemingway Av.
East Haven, CT 06512

Mr. Paperback
123 Foster Parkway East
Fort Wayne, IN 46852

The Plains Distrib. Services
P.O. Box 3112 – Room 406
Fargo, ND 58102

Publishers Services
6318 Vesper Av.
Van Nuys, CA 91411

Quality Books, Inc.
918 Sherwood Dr.
Lake Bluff, IL 60044

Small Press Distribution
1814 San Pablo Av.
Berkely, CA 94702

Retail Bookstore Chains: One of the best ways to sell your book
is to interest one of the larger bookstore chains. They are in the
envious position to move hundreds of copies of your book through
display and promotion. Like everything else, it's not easy but worth
a try. The larger chains are;

Crown Discount Books
3301 Pennsy Drive
Landover, MD 20785
(about 100 stores)

Dalton Booksellers
One Corporate Center
7505 Metro Blvd.
Minneapolis, MN 55435
(about 595 outlets including
Pickwick Discount stores)

Follett Corp.
1000 W. Washington Blvd.
Chicago, IL 60607
(220 College Bookstores)

Kroch's & Bretano's
29 South Wabash Ave.
Chicago, IL 60603
(About 20 stores)

Waldenbooks (owned by K Mart)
201 High Ridge Rd.
Stanford, CT 06904
(about 1,000 stores)

Practically every department store now has a book section. If you convince the book buyers for the large chains (Sears, J.C. Penney, Montgomery Ward, K Mart, Venture, etc.) to handle your book, you could sell hundreds or even thousands of copies. The largest bookstore in the world is Barnes & Noble, 105 Fifth Avenue, N.Y.C., NY 10003.

Another source for the mass sales of books is through the Book-of-the-Month Club, 485 Lexington Avenue, N.Y.C., NY 10017. Not only do they select one book of the month, but they also issue a monthly catalog of other books to sell to members.

Professional Book Promotion Services: In order for your book to sell, it must be exposed to the book buying public. Professional book promotion services are available to the self-publishing author. The services can be productive and can create a demand for your book. Write for details and cost.

Benn Hall Associates, 430 Lexington Ave., Suite 3102, N.Y.C., NY 10017; offers a publicity service for books written by unknown authors and printed in small quantity editions.

The Bookers, 200 W. 51st St., N.Y.C., NY 10019; book promotion services specializing in television and radio interviews.

Cahners Books, 89 Franklin St., Boston, MA 02110; displays books at business shows.

Canaan Communications, Inc., 310 East 44th St., N.Y.C., NY 10017; book promotions.

Kampman and Co., 9 East 40th St., N.Y.C., NY 10016; promotes and distributes books for small publishers.

Janice Morgan Communications, 301 W. 53rd St., Apt. 13B, N.Y.C., NY 10019; book publicity services.

Morton Dennis Wax and Assoc., 1560 Broadway, N.Y.C., NY 10036; book promotion for newly published books.

Rex Communications, Inc., 150 Fifth Ave., N.Y.C., NY 10011; offers publicity for books and authors on 100 talk shows without the necessity of personal appearances.

Roth Advertising, 125 Mineola Av., Roslyn Heights, N.Y. 11577; handles advertising and promotion of new books.

Selma Shapiro, 501 Fifth Av., Suite 500, N.Y.C., NY 10017; book promotions.

Annette Swanberg, 7424 W. 81st St., Los Angeles, CA 90045; book promotions.

Irwin Zucker, 6430 Sunset Blvd., Hollywood, CA 90028; promotes books, publicizes authors, and publishes a monthly bulletin of book news.

Book Mailing and Shipping Services: If you are unable to undertake the warehousing, packing and mailing of your books, hire a firm to handle these operations for you. Here are firms specializing in this type of service for book publishers:

Harte-Hanks Fulfillment
25 John Rd.
Canton, MA 02021

J. V. Co.
P.O. Box 11950
Reno, NV 89510

Krakow, Inc.
8748 Remmet Av.
Canoga Park, CA 91304

Mid-Atlantic Book Service
5 Laurence St.
Bloomfield, NJ 07003

Professional Book Distrib.
2727 Scioto Pkwy.
Columbus, OH 43220

Publishers Marketing Services
11661 San Vincente Blvd. – 206
Los Angeles, CA 90049

Publishers Systems, Inc.
54 Warehouse Lane
Rowley, MA 01969

W. A. Book Service, Inc.
26 Ranich Rd.
Hauppauge, NY 11787

Miscellaneous Information

How To Send Books Through The Mails: If you plan to mail books to customers, you will need proper mailing envelopes or padded book shipping bags. Envelopes with clasps are suitable for the mailing of paperbacks, and should be of durable 28 lb. or 32 lb. brown kraft material. For the mailing of thin books, the envelope should be about ½ inch wider and ½ inch longer than the book. A 5½x8½ book should be mailed in a 6x9 envelope, a 5x7 book in a 5½x7½ envelope, etc. If your paperback book is thick, it may require a larger size mailing envelope. For mailing of hard covered books or very thick paperbacks, use padded book shipping bags which come in various sizes depending upon the size of your book. Envelopes and book shipping bags can be purchased in smaller quantities from an office supply store. For quantity purchases, see next paragraph.

A manufacturer that makes practically any size book mailing envelope is Accurate Envelope Company, 320 Lafayette St., N.Y.C., NY 10012. For padded book shipping bags, contact either Jiffy Manufacturing Co., 560 Central Av. Murray Hill, NJ 07974 or Columbian Rope Co., Auburn, NY 13021. These firms may not sell you direct but will advise you of the closest distributor from whom the envelopes or bags may be ordered.

You will also need shipping labels which can be ordered, printed with your name and address, from a local print shop.

Books that meet designated specifications can be sent through the mails at a special low rate of postage. Books of 24 or more pages, at least 22 of which are printed, permanently bound, consisting wholly of reading matter, and containing no advertising other than incidental announcement of books, are eligible for these postal rates. It is necessary to endorse the mailing wrapper "Special Fourth Class Rate—Contents: Book" in order to take advantage of these rates. Thus, a book weighing 1½ pounds including the weight of the mailing envelope or shipping bag, can be sent anywhere in the United States for 94¢ postage. If the same book were sent regular parcel post without the endorsement, the postage to the eighth zone would be $2.30. Multiply this saving by 1,000 or 2,000 books and you can see how much you can reduce your book shipping cost. Postal rates are constantly changing so check with your post office for current book mailing rates.

What To Do With Unsold Copies: You might try donating them to a charitable organization and taking an income tax deduction as a contribution. A number of companies buy remainder stocks of books from publishers and other sources. They don't pay much, but what good are books that have no possibility of reaching the public? Here are some firms that purchase "remainder" copies:

Book Sales, Inc.
110 Enterprise Av.
Saucaucus, NJ 07094

Book World Promotions, Inc.
87-93 Christie St.
Newark, NJ 07105

Bookseller
30-4 Chambers
Danbury, CT 06810

Booksmith Promotions
432 Park Av. S
N.Y.C., NY 10016

Bookthrift, Inc.
45 W. 36th St.
N.Y.C., NY 10018

Marboro Books
122 Fifth Av. at 18th
N.Y.C., NY 10011

Outlet Book Co.
225 Park Av. S
N.Y.C., NY 10003

Overstock Book Co. Inc.
120 Secatogue Av.
Farmingdale, NY 11735

Quality Books
918 Sherwood Dr.
Lake Bluff, IL 60044

X-S Books, Inc.
725 Dell Rd.
Carlstadt, NJ 07072

Joining A Writers' Association: As a published or unpublished author, you may desire to affiliate yourself with an organization of writers. For membership information, contact the club direct.

American Society of Journalists
   and Authors, Inc.
1501 Broadway
N.Y.C., NY 10036

Authors League of America, Inc.
234 W. 44th St.
N.Y.C., NY 10036

The National Writers Club
1450 S. Havana
Aurora, CO 80012

Poets and Writers
201 W. 54th St.
N.Y.C., NY 10019

P.E.N. – American Center
568 Broadway
N.Y.C., NY 10012

Associations for Self-Publishing Authors:

Cosmep, Inc., P.O. Box 703, San Francisco, CA 94101 ($45 yr.)

Marin Self-Publishers Assn., P.O. Box 1346, Ross, CA 94957 ($18 yr.)

National Assn. of Independent Publishers, P.O. Box 850, Moore Haven, FL 33471 ($50 yr.)

Pascal, 2401 Pacific Coast Hwy, Hermosa, Beach, CA 90254 ($75 + yr.)

Writers Magazines and Publications: Every potential author should subscribe to at least one of the leading writer's magazines. Each issue contains helpful articles on writing and information on how to market the material you write. Personal experiences of authors makes interesting reading.

General magazines for writers:

The Writer
120 Boylston St.
Boston, MA 02116
(circulation – 57,000 –
monthly – $19 yr.)

Writer's Digest
9933 Alliance Rd.
Cincinnati, OH 45242
(circulation – 200,000 –
monthly – $21 yr.)

Of special interest to self-publishers:

Cosmep Newsletter
P.O. Box 703
San Francisco, CA 94101
(monthly – $45 yr.)

Small Press Review
Box 100
Paradise, CA 95969
(circulation – 3,000 –
monthly – $16 yr.)

Small Press
11 Ferry Lane West
Westport, CT 06880
(circulation – 9,000 –
bi-monthly – $19.95)

Annual publications of interest to writers:

Literary Market Place
205 E. 42nd St.
N.Y.C., NY 10017
(the Business Directory of
Book Publishing – $75.00)

Writer's Handbook
120 Boylston St.
Boston, MA 02116
(Writing instruction and
markets – 780 pages – $24.94)

Writer's Market
9933 Alliance Rd.
Cincinnati, OH 45242
(Marketing information—
1060 pages—$19.95)

Writer's Yearbook
9933 Alliance Rd.
Cincinnati, OH 45242
(For beginning and
professional writers—$3.95

Getting Funds for Self-Publishing: It is possible, under certain conditions, to get money in the form of government or private grants to pay for the publication of books or magazines. It is not easy, and you may have to meet some stringent criteria to become eligible for these grants. However, tens of thousands of dollars are allocated each year to small non-profit book and magazine publishers.

First, find out what grants are available in your own state. Contact your senator or representative to determine what funds have been allocated for this purpose and how to apply.

One of the best booklets on the subject is *Grants and Awards Available to American Writers* ($6) and can be secured from P.E.N. American Center, 568 Broadway, N.Y.C., NY 10012. Another is *The Foundation Directory* ($65) available from The Foundation Center, 79 Fifth Avenue, N.Y.C., NY 10003. Also write to The Foundation Center for their catalog of other related books that are available.

Information can also be secured from the National Endowment For The Arts, 1100 Pennsylvania Ave. N.W., Washington, D.C. 20506; and from the Coordinating Council of Literary Magazines, 2 Park Ave., N.Y.C., NY 10016.

Your Status for Income Tax Purposes: The printing and sales of books as a self-publisher is considered a business (either full or part time) and Uncle Sam expects you to pay income taxes on any profit made above the cost of producing your book. On the other hand, should your venture end in a loss, you can deduct the amount of your loss from other income you received during the year. It is essential that you keep accurate records of all costs as well as income. Expenses include the cost of printing, copyright fee, typing fees, advertising, stationery, and postage costs. In addition you can deduct the cost of travel to and from lecture tours for the purpose of plugging your book, membership fees in professional (writers) organizations, and all other expenses directly connected with the promotion or sale of your book.

Under certain circumstances, you might also be able to deduct a share of your household expenses if your book was written in your home or if you maintain an office in your home for distribution of your books. Consult a tax accountant for assistance in the preparation of your return. In order to report your profit or deduct your losses, you will be required to file Schedule C, Income or Loss From Profession or Business.

The simplest method of bookkeeping is to compute the cost of each book. Let us assume that the original cost of producing 1,000 copies of your book was $2,000. This figures to $2 per copy. If you sold your book for $4 each and you were able to sell 200 copies a year, your sales income would be $800. Deducting the cost of the 200 books (at $2 per book), the cost of sales would amount to $400, leaving a gross profit of $400. From this gross profit would be deducted all expenses incurred during the year in connection with promoting the book, and other expenses relating to the selling of the books. Let us say that these expenses amounted to $250; you would then have made a profit of $150 on which you would be required to pay income tax. If the expenses amounted to $485, you would have suffered a loss of $85 which is deductible from other income subject to tax. If you are finally stuck with books that you can no longer sell, the cost of these books added to any expenses as enumerated above is fully deductible in the final year.

Two helpful and free books are available from your local Internal Revenue Service Office. *Your Federal Income Tax* (Publication 17); and *Tax Guide for Small Business* (Publication 334).

Also check if your state requires the payment of sales taxes on books sold at retail.

Miscellaneous Notes: If you plan to have a book printed, don't wait. With production costs on the rise, the longer you wait, the more you will pay ... There are about 670,000 book titles now in print by 18,000 publishers. 45,000 new titles are issued each year ... The reading public now spends about five million dollars a year to buy books ... The *average* novel sells for about $15 a copy in the hard cover edition ... There are approximately 80,000 retail outlets for books in this country ... In order for a paperback book to be considered a "best seller" it must sell from 200,000 to two million copies.

For self-publishing authors, the easiest books to sell are the "How To" books. Eager readers are buying such books as "How to Buy and Operate a Computer," "How to Get the Most out of your Word Processor," "How to Get Rich in Mail Order," "How to Make Money in the Stock Market," "How to Find a Husband (or Wife)," and "How to Control Diabetes (or High Blood Pressure, or Arthritis)." Also note the title of the book you are now reading . . . Genealogy books have always had a ready market and sell at higher prices than most other books . . . Historical, political, and religious non-fiction books are good sellers . . . Fiction novels are difficult to market, and the hardest books to sell are books of poetry.

The most common error that authors make is the misspelling of the word "FOREWORD" . . . And make sure that your copyright notice, Library of Congress catalog card number, and ISBN appear on the back of your title page . . . A page is considered one side of the sheet; the printing on the back is another page . . . We repeat: The odd numbered pages 1, 3, 5, 7, etc. are *always* printed on the right hand side of the sheet; 2, 4, 6, 8, etc. are printed on the left side of the sheet (on the back of the odd numbered pages).

For an art designed cover or dust jacket, contact Trapkus Art Studio, 5120 11th Avenue C, Moline, IL 61265. He can also prepare an effective ad for your advertising . . . To have from one to fifty copies of your paperback book bound in hard covers, contact Dierkes Bindery, P.O. Box 509, Eureka Springs, AR 72632 . . . An editing and proofreading service is provided by Jean B. Bernard, 1717 Lanier Rd. N.W., Washington, D.C. 20009 . . . Two successful self-publishing authors who offer to help other authors promote their books are Dan Poynter, Para Publishing, P.O. Box 4232, Santa Barbara, CA 93140; and Jerry Buchanan, Towers Club, P.O. Box 2038, Vancouver, WA 98668.

If yours is a genealogy book, the best place to advertise is in the leading publication in the field, *The Genealogical Helper,* P.O. Box 368, Logan, UT 84321 (circulation 49,000 – bi-monthly – $17 yr.) Also send them a copy of your book for a review in their publication . . . The largest seller of genealogical books is Godspeed's Book Shop, 7 Beacon St., Boston, MA 02108. They issue a catalog ($5) listing over 2300 individual family histories which they carry in stock . . . A distributor of genealogy books is Heritage Distribution Center, P.O. Box 22125, Denver, CO 80222 . . . Family Histories, Genealogical Society of Utah, 50 East North Terrace, Salt Lake City, UT 84150, has a large collection of family histories and may be interested in adding yours . . . A catalog of *Genealogical and Local History Books in Print* (1700 pages in two volumes) is available from Genealogical Books in Print, 6818 Lois Dr., Springfield, VA 22150. You can also have your book listed at a nominal charge.

If poetry is your specialty and you would like to have your book reviewed or listed, send for a copy of *International Directory of Little Magazines and Small Presses* ($19.95) available from Dustbooks, Box 100, Paradise, CA 95969 . . . Information on 22,000 contemporary American poets and writers is available from Poets and Writers, 201 W. 54th St., N.Y.C., NY 10019 . . . The two leading poetry magazines are *American Poetry Review,* Center City, 1616 Walnut St., Room 405, Philadelphia, PA 19103 (circulation 24,000 — bi-monthly — $7.50 yr.); and *Poetry,* Box 4348, 601 S. Morgan St., Chicago, IL 60680 (circulation 6,000 — $22 yr.) . . . An association of poets is the Poetry Society of America, 15 Gramercy Park, N.Y.C., NY 10003 (1300 members).

You can find tremendous savings on the purchase of popular books by writing for the *Publishers Closeouts Catalog* from Publishers Central Bureau, One Champion Ave., Avenel, NJ 07001 . . . Buy all your books and current magazines at discounts (even the best sellers) at one of the many hundreds of Crown Discount Book Stores . . . Get your magazine subscriptions at wholesale by writing to McGregor Subscription Agency, Mount Vernon, IL 60154. Make money by soliciting subscriptions from friends, relatives and others and placing them through McGregor at wholesale.

The Truth About "Subsidy" Publishers

In recent years, a number of firms have come into existence offering to publish books on a "subsidy" or "co-operative" basis. The "publisher" implies that he will share the expense of publication with the author, that many copies of the book will be sold, that "royalties" will be paid, and that the author will not only recoup his initial investment, but will make a profit as well. Competition became so keen among these firms that more and more irrational statements were made and more and more gullible authors were taken in by the forceful and impressive literature sent out by these firms. So many complaints were filed with various Better Business Bureaus and government agencies, that the Federal Trade Commission stepped in and issued Cease and Desist orders against many of the "vanity" publishers. While these firms are still going strong, and their ads appear in many publications, prospective customers should check the facts before signing any contracts for publication.

If you would like to receive a factual report of the operations of "subsidy" publishers, or of any specific "subsidy" publisher, send your request to the Better Business Bureau of New York City, Inc., 257 Park Ave. S, N.Y.C., NY 10010. In addition, write to the Federal Trade Commission, Washington, D.C. 20540, requesting a copy of the "Complaint" and "Decision" filed against any specific "subsidy" publisher. Also send a stamped self-addressed long envelope to *Writer's Digest*, 9933 Alliance Road, Cincinnati, OH 45242, for a free reprint of *Should You Pay To Have It Published? The Writer,* one of the most distinguished magazines for writers, refuses to accept advertising from "subsidy" publishers.

Many articles and books have been written by disillusioned authors about their experiences with "subsidy" publishers. One author has even written a book to tell in detail what happened when he signed a "contract" to have his book "published." Although the book, *The New Author's Dilemma* has been sold out and is no longer available, permission has been received from the author, Edward A. Dobran, to reprint his introduction.

Introduction from "The New Author's Dilemma"
by Edward A. Dobran

(reprinted with permission of the author)

Although experience is the best teacher it is often costly. This manual was composed from the notes of such experience in the literary field over a period of years. It was especially compiled on behalf of new unpublished authors, who are seeking a competent publisher for their literary works.

The literary career is too frequently looked upon as the most attractive and simplest to succeed in—not until one has tried to succeed in this field himself, though, does he realize differently. No one but an author can imagine the tension, heartbreak and discouragement that is involved in literary work.

The chances the new, unpublished writer has at getting his works published today may appear somewhat easier now than formerly. The explanation for this, of course, is that many authors have turned to subsidizing their works through a growing but insecure plan which is practiced regularly by co-operative publishers. The plan as advertised, requires a minimal subsidy from the author. Under such a plan, the author gets his works published. Apart from being bound to an unfair contract, that's about the limit of it. So far as a decent amount of profit or prestige is concerned, this is practically out of the question, under such a plan.

Although a considerable number of notables in the literary field have gained success and recognition through subsidizing their first works, do not confuse the methods they use with those practiced by the co-operative publishers. Most of such an author's success can be credited to the individual's own will to succeed. The majority of such authors practically acted as publisher, promoter and salesman for their own works. The achievements of these notables, however, serves as a splendid example for the subsidy publisher to point to when trying to induce new authors to patronize their publishing house.

The promotional literature sent out to authors by such publishers is always cleverly worded. If the author is not completely alert, he will be under the impression that a similar subsidy plan is responsible for the success of mentioned notables.

So far as the subsidy or so-called co-operative publisher is concerned, it is difficult to distinguish the competent or legitimate publisher from the deceiving fraud.

It is not the intent of this manual to slander or incriminate the activities of any co-operative publisher who is competent and legitimate. This manual is strictly directed to those publishers whom the shoe may fit. If any publishers may be in doubt – try the shoe for size and let their consciences be their guides.

The literary field is jam-packed with various literary people other than just conniving publishers, many of whom lurk behind impressive titles as literary agents, advertising agencies, book clubs, etc. Regardless of the title they assume, these ruthless swindlers are constantly alert to taking financial advantage of an author at any time.

Whether an author's profession is that of teacher, physician, clergyman, businessman or some other, he is not excluded from the possibility of falling prey to the crafty tactics of these trained literary leeches!

It is the sincere hope of the writer of this advisory guide to give the reader a general preview of the deceiving tactics practiced by these literary con-men, and to establish a stronger conclusive form of decision in the minds of every literary-minded person, that he may be in a position to interpret better any proposals offered by the "unnnecessary evils" which prowl the literary field today.

HOW WOULD YOU LIKE THIS TO HAPPEN TO YOUR BOOK?

A Fairfax County Virginia seventh-grader came home from school this week with a limited-edition copy of "The Short Season," a biography of Brian Piccolo, the Chicago Bears football star who died of leukemia.

For 96 pages, she read the account of Piccolo's short but courageous life and a trip he had been offered to the Bahamas when she suddenly found herself getting tips on "How to drive a man to ecstasy" and "How to tell a good bed prospect" – chapters that had nothing at all to do with Piccolo.

As a result of an error in the automated book-binding process, explained the publishing firm's spokesman, the life of Piccolo and 2½ chapters of "The Sensuous Woman" by "J" wound up between the same paperback covers.

"This is very embarrassing and we're very sorry it happened," said a spokesman for the printer.

Copy of complaint filed against "X", a "vanity" publisher
before the Federal Trade Commission, August 5, 1958

PARAGRAPH TWO: Respondents are now and for more than two years last past have been engaged in the solicitation of contracts for the publication of books for authors and prospective authors and in the promotion, sale and distribution of books of authors, contracting with respondents. Said solicitations are made through advertisements placed in magazines, periodicals and newspapers, and otherwise, all of which are circulated to authors and prospective authors located in various states of the United States and in the District of Columbia.

PARAGRAPH FOUR: In the course and conduct of their said business in commerce, by means of brochures and other letters, postal cards, circulars and through advertisements, as aforesaid, respondents invite authors to send their manuscripts to respondents for an appraisal of their literary merit and sales potential.

Upon receipt, the manuscript is assigned to a reader to read, after which a letter is composed to the submitting author. Except in rare instances, this letter gives a praiseworthy appraisal of the manuscript and recommends it for publication; said letter also contains various statements relating to the sales promotion and publicity respondents propose to place behind the book. A contract is generally enclosed for execution and provides for payment of a specific sum in one or more installments, all of which must be paid before the manuscript in book form is released for sale.

PARAGRAPH FIVE: In the course and conduct of their business as aforesaid, respondents have made many statements and representations, directly or indirectly, concerning the nature, size and operation of their said business, the sales, promotion and publicity afforded their author customers and the effectiveness of same and results obtained thereby. Typical, but not all-inclusive of said statements and representations, are the following:

1. That theirs is a cooperative publishing plan in which respondents share with the author in the expense of the editing, printing, binding, publication, promotion and sale of the book and that respondents are partners with the author;

2. The respondents publish on a partial subsidy basis;

3. That under respondents' plan of publication, the author recovers his entire investment in the publication of his or her book very soon after its publication and well before a sell-out of the first edition;

4. That respondents bind all the copies of the first edition of the book listed in the contract with the author;

5. That respondents have a large organization with numerous employees and departments, including an art department;

6. That respondents only accept for publication those manuscripts having merit and sales appeal and that manuscripts accepted by them have been determined to have such merit and sales appeal before respondents will risk their own money in publishing said manuscript;

7. That respondents have a board of editors who examine each author's work carefully and report impartially, fully and frankly on its literary merit and sales potential;

8. That respondents have publicity and promotion departments which conduct intelligent and effective promotion and sales campaigns of their authors' books, and that the same reach some 6,400 book trade outlets in North America;

9. That respondents reinforce their sales promotion of their authors' books with extensive national-direct mail drives;

10. The respondents' sales department is in constant touch with retail bookstores, libraries, universities, wholesalers and department stores, all of which repeatedly buy the books published by respondents;

11. That respondents sell and have sold reprint rights in their authors' books to pocket book reprint companies; that respondents' authors' books published through respondents have been selected by book clubs for sale to the book club members; and that respondents sell and have sold their authors' books published through respondents to book clubs and to book club members;

12. That respondents sell, and have sold, subsidiary rights to their authors' books published through respondents, to foreign publishers, television producers, motion picture studios, digest and serialized periodicals;

13. That respondents pay their authors a 40% royalty;

14. That respondents arrange for reviews of their authors' books in key periodicals;

15. That respondents offer an exclusive book service;

16. That respondents have never sold any selected poetry, Christian or fiction books at reduced prices for lack of continuing sales;

17. That respondents are accredited with all large book wholesalers, jobbers and retail outlets.

PARAGRAPH SIX: **The aforesaid statements and representations are false, misleading and deceptive.** In truth and in fact:

1. Respondents do not operate a cooperative publishing plan in that they do not share with the author in the expense of editing, printing, binding, publication, promotion and sale of the book, nor are they partners with the author; in truth and in fact, the sum charged an author by respondents, except in rare instances, covers the entire expense of editing, printing, binding, publishing, promotion, distributing and selling the finished book, plus a profit to respondents;

2. Respondents do not publish on a partial subsidy basis but require a complete subsidy covering the entire cost of publishing and promotion of the author's book;

3. The author seldom recovers more than a small amount of the money paid respondents at any time, let alone the entire investment. In truth and in fact, only in rare and exceptional cases do any of said books sell-out the entire first edition;

4. Respondents do not bind all of the copies of an author's first edition of the book respondents contract to publish and often bind less than half the number of copies called for in the contract;

5. Respondents do not have a large organization with numerous employees and departments, nor do they have an art department;

59

6. Respondents accept, and have accepted for publication, manuscripts which do not have merit or sales appeal possibilities and their experience has been such that they knew or should have known that many of the manuscripts they accept have neither merit nor sales appeal possibilities. In truth and in fact, respondents do not "risk" their own money in publishing an author's manuscript as the sum paid by the author to respondents covers all cost plus a profit thereon to respondents;

7. Respondents do not have a board of editors. Respondents employ readers to read the manuscripts and report on same; such reports are neither impartial, full nor frank disclosures of the merit or sales potential of the submitted manuscript; said report is written in glowing and laudatory terms for the purpose of convincing the author that the manuscript has literary merit and sales potential and should be published.

8. Respondents do not have publicity and promotion departments; respondents' publicity promotion campaigns do not reach any significant number of book trade outlets in North America;

9. Respondents do not reinforce the sales promotion of their authors' books with national direct mail drives;

10. Respondents do not have a sales department. Their dealings with retail book stores, libraries, universities, wholesalers or department stores are limited. Such outlets buy few of the books published by respondents.

11. None of the books published through respondents have been selected by book clubs for sale to, nor have same been sold to, a book club or a book club's membership, nor have they sold the reprint rights of any book to pocket book reprint companies;

12. Respondents do not sell, nor have they sold, subsidiary rights to their authors' books published through respondents to foreign publishers, television producers, motion picture studios, digest or periodicals;

13. Respondents do not pay their authors a 40% royalty or any kind of royalty. Respondents' plan of publication is one whereby the author subsidizes the publication of his or her book with the author paying for the entire cost of same, plus a profit to respondents in practically all cases. Respondents agree to pay the author 40% on the sales price of all the author's books sold and paid for, but only in rare cases are the sales ever sufficient for the author to recoup his or her investment made with respondents for the publication, promotion and sale of the author's book;

14. Respondents do not arrange for reviews of their authors' books in key periodicals;

15. Respondents do not offer an author an exclusive book service, and in truth and in fact, the respondents' service does not differ from that of other subsidy publishers;

16. Respondents have sold poetry, Christian and fiction books at reduced prices for lack of continued sales;

17. Respondents are accredited with few, if any, large book wholesalers, jobbers or retail outlets.

An individual's carriage, poise, build, complexion, clothes, facial expressions all play important parts in making up one's personality. The most striking thing about an individual's personal appearance is his clothes. Clothes do not make the man, but they do make impressions, good or bad. We have some control over some items which make up our personal appearance. Little can we do about weight at times, except carry ourselves well. We have more control over weight than height. Posture can be controlled to a certain extent. IF AN INDIVIDUAL IS CARELESS ABOUT HIS PERSON, HE IS APT TO BE CARELESS ABOUT HIS THINKING AND DOING.

Expressions are important in personality. Voice is perhaps the most fluent medium through which individuals express their personalities. Frequently, what is said is secondary in importance to how it is said. Voice is our social passport. Impressions are gained quickly from the way an individual expresses himself. Language is the dress of thought. One's tone, pitch, inflection of voice and his speed and ease of talking, play an important part in other people's attitude toward him. One's verbal habits reflect largely his thinking habits.

The quality of an individual's intelligence is determined largely by his ability to reason clearly, to think quickly and to judge values properly. Intelligence is judged mostly by an individual's thinking rather than by his ability to recall facts. How an individual uses his intelligence, depends largely upon his training. Education is too often mistaken

---

This page was prepared on an IBM Selectric II typewriter, Bookface Academic #72 type, for a 5½x8½ book. It was typed in an area of 4¼x7 inches, and is printed the same size as typed without reduction.

An individual's carriage, poise, build, complexion, clothes, facial expressions all play important parts in making up one's personality. The most striking thing about an individual's personal appearance is his clothes. Clothes do not make the man, but they do make impressions, good or bad. We have some control over some items which make up our personal appearance. Little can we do about weight at times, except carry ourselves well. We have more control over weight than height. Posture can be controlled to a certain extent. IF AN INDIVIDUAL IS CARELESS ABOUT HIS PERSON, HE IS APT TO BE CARELESS ABOUT HIS THINKING AND DOING.

Expressions are important in personality. Voice is perhaps the most fluent medium through which individuals express their personalities. Frequently, what is said is secondary in importance to how it is said. Voice is our social passport. Impressions are gained quickly from the way an individual expresses himself. Language is the dress of thought. One's tone, pitch, inflection of voice and his speed and ease of talking, play an important part in other people's attitude toward him. One's verbal habits reflect largely his thinking habits.

The quality of an individual's intelligence is determined largely by his ability to reason clearly, to think quickly and to judge values properly. Intelligence is judged mostly by an individual's thinking rather than by his ability to recall facts. How an individual uses his intelligence, depends largely upon his training. Education is too often mistaken for intelligence.

This page was prepared in the same area as the previous page except that lines were justified (even right hand margin).

An individual's carriage, poise, build, complexion, clothes, facial expressions all play important parts in making up one's personality. The most striking thing about an individual's personal appearance is his clothes. Clothes do not make the man, but they do make impressions, good or bad. We have some control over some items which make up our personal appearance. Little can we do about weight at times, except carry ourselves well. We have more control over weight than height. Posture can be controlled to a certain extent. IF AN INDIVIDUAL IS CARELESS ABOUT HIS PERSON, HE IS APT TO BE CARELESS ABOUT HIS THINKING AND DOING.

Expressions are important in personality. Voice is perhaps the most fluent medium through which individuals express their personalities. Fre- quently, what is said is secondary in importance to how it is said. Voice is our social passport. Impressions are gained quickly from the way an individual expresses himself. Language is the dress of thought. One's tone, pitch, inflection of voice and his speed and ease of talking, play an important part in other people's attitude toward him. One's verbal habits reflect largely his thinking habits.

The quality of an individual's intelligence is determined largely by his ability to reason clearly, to think quickly and to judge values properly. Intelligence is judged mostly by an individual's thinking rather than by his ability to recall facts. How an individual uses his intelligence, depends largely upon his training. Education is too often mistaken for intelligence.

Thought is one of the most important tools of intelligence. It is a tool with which we master our lives and the lives of others. As a man thinketh—so is he. Every person has some train of thought that molds and makes him what he is. One becomes great as he grows with the power to think and put useful thought into action. Reason is the sharp chisel that carves out thought. Intelligence controls all the incidents of an individual's life and most of the reactions he

---

This page was prepared on an IBM Selectric II typewriter, Bookface Academic #72 type for a 5½x8½ book. It was typed in an area of 4¾x7¾ inches and reduced by 10% before printing.

An individual's carriage, poise, build, complexion, clothes, facial expressions all play important parts in making up one's personality. The most striking thing about an individual's personal appearance is his clothes. Clothes do not make the man, but they do make impressions, good or bad. We have some control over some items which make up our personal appearance. Little can we do about weight at times, except carry ourselves well. We have more control over weight than height. Posture can be controlled to a certain extent. IF AN INDIVIDUAL IS CARELESS ABOUT HIS PERSON, HE IS APT TO BE CARELESS ABOUT HIS THINKING AND DOING.

Expressions are important in personality. Voice is perhaps the most fluent medium through which individuals express their personalities. Frequently, what is said is secondary in importance to how it is said. Voice is our social passport. Impressions are gained quickly from the way an individual expresses himself. Language is the dress of thought. One's tone, pitch, inflection of voice and his speed and ease of talking, play an important part in other people's attitude toward him. One's verbal habits reflect largely his thinking habits.

The quality of an individual's intelligence is determined largely by his ability to reason clearly, to think quickly and to judge values properly. Intelligence is judged mostly by an individual's thinking rather than by his ability to recall facts. How an individual uses his intelligence, depends largely upon his training. Education is too often mistaken for intelligence.

Thought is one of the most important tools of intelligence. It is a tool with which we master our lives and the lives of others. As a man thinketh—so is he. Every person has some train of thought that molds and makes him what he is. One becomes great as he grows with the power to think and put useful thought into action. Reason is the sharp chisel that carves out thought. Intelligence controls all the incidents of an individual's life and most of the reactions he makes to the world about him.

Manners of walking, standing and sitting; manners of expression, gestures, and speech; and many other little traits of character are betrayed

---

This page was prepared on an IBM Selectric II typewriter, Bookface Academic #72 type, for a 5½x8½ book. It was typed in an area of 5x8½ inches and reduced by 15% before printing.

An individual's carriage, poise, build, complexion, clothes, facial expressions all play important parts in making up one's personality. The most striking thing about an individual's personal appearance is his clothes. Clothes do not make the man, but they do make impressions, good or bad. We have some control over some items which make up our personal appearance. Little can we do about weight at times, except carry ourselves well. We have more control over weight than height. Posture can be controlled to a certain extent. IF AN INDIVIDUAL IS CARELESS ABOUT HIS PERSON, HE IS APT TO BE CARELESS ABOUT HIS THINKING AND DOING.

Expressions are important in personality. Voice is perhaps the most fluent medium through which individuals express their personalities. Frequently, what is said is secondary in importance to how it is said. Voice is our social passport. Impressions are gained quickly from the way an individual expresses himself. Language is the dress of thought. One's tone, pitch, inflection of voice and his speed and ease of talking, play an important part in other people's attitude toward him. One's verbal habits reflect largely his thinking habits.

The quality of an individual's intelligence is determined largely by his ability to reason clearly, to think quickly and to judge values properly. Intelligence is judged mostly by an individual's thinking rather than by his ability to recall facts. How an individual uses his intelligence, depends largely upon his training. Education is too often mistaken for intelligence.

Thought is one of the most important tools of intelligence. It is a tool with which we master our lives and the lives of others. As a man thinketh—so is he. Every person has some train of thought that molds and makes him what he is. One becomes great as he grows with the power to think and put useful thought into action. Reason is the sharp chisel that carves out thought. Intelligence controls all the incidents of an individual's life and most of the reactions he makes to the world about him.

Manners of walking, standing and sitting; manners of expression, gestures, and speech; and many other little traits of character are betrayed by an individual's appearance.

Every normal individual can control his essential points of appearance. The fact that he is tall or short, handsome or ugly may be beyond control, but he certainly can see to it that he is neat and clean;

This page was prepared on an IBM Selectric II typewriter, Bookface Academic #72 type, for a 5½x8½ book. It was typed in an area of 5½x8¾ inches and reduced by 20% before printing.

An individual's carriage, poise, build, complexion, clothes, facial expressions all play important parts in making up one's personality. The most striking thing about an individual's personal appearance is his clothes. *Clothes do not make the man,* but they do make impressions, good or bad. We have some control over some items which make up our personal appearance. Little can we do about weight at times, except carry ourselves well. We have more control over weight than height. Posture can be controlled to a certain extent. IF AN INDIVIDUAL IS CARELESS ABOUT HIS PERSON, HE IS APT TO BE CARELESS ABOUT HIS THINKING AND DOING.

Expressions are important in personality. Voice is perhaps the most fluent medium through which individuals express their personalities. Frequently, what is said is secondary in importance to how it is said. Voice is our social passport. Impressions are gained quickly from the way an individual expresses himself. *Language is the dress of thought.* One's tone, pitch, inflection of voice and his speed and ease of talking, play an important part in other people's attitude toward him. One's verbal habits reflect largely his thinking habits.

The quality of an individual's intelligence is determined largely by his ability to reason clearly, to think quickly and to judge values properly. Intelligence is judged mostly by an individual's thinking rather than by his ability to recall facts. How an individual uses his intelligence, depends largely upon his training. Education is too often mistaken for intelligence.

Thought is one of the most important tools of intelligence. It is a tool with which we master our lives and the lives of others. *As a man thinketh—so is he.* Every person has some train of thought that molds and makes him what he is. One becomes great as he grows with the power to think and put useful thought into action. Reason is the sharp chisel that carves out thought. Intelligence controls all the incidents of an individual's life and most of the reactions he makes to the world about him.

Manners of walking, standing and sitting; manners of expression, gestures, and speech; and many other little traits of character are betrayed by an individual's appearance.

Every normal individual can control his essential points of appearance. The fact that he is tall or short, handsome or ugly may be beyond control, but he certainly can see to it

---

This page is typeset by the printer in Century book type for a 5½x8½ book. Italics and bold face type are also available.

This Photo Has
Been Screened

Same Photo
That Has Not
Been Screened

INFORMATION SLIP

Description of new book for FREE record in Cumulative Book Index, published by
The H. W. Wilson Company, 950 University Ave., Bronx, N.Y. 10452

The Cumulative Book Index is published monthly.   A copy of the book or descriptive
material will be appreciated.

Author ....
    (Full Name) (Please print)

Title ....
    (Verbatim)

....

Subject ....

Series and Number ....

Edition......... No. of vols....... Size........ No. of pages........ Illustrations........

Binding .... Retail price........... Date of publication ....
    (In your currency)   (Exact)

Name and Address of Publisher ....
    (From whom the book may be obtained)

For *IMPORTATIONS* the following additional information is *REQUIRED:* (a) Are you the sole U.S.
agent for the book? .... (b) What is the U.S. publication date? ....; (c) How many copies
will be on hand in this country on the U.S. publication date? (or are on hand now)? ....

11-65—50M(2687)M.A. Printed in U.S.A.

(See Page 23)

68

FORM TX

UNITED STATES COPYRIGHT OFFICE

REGISTRATION NUMBER

TX _____ TXU

EFFECTIVE DATE OF REGISTRATION

_____ _____ _____
Month   Day   Year

DO NOT WRITE ABOVE THIS LINE. IF YOU NEED MORE SPACE, USE A SEPARATE CONTINUATION SHEET.

1 TITLE OF THIS WORK ▼

PREVIOUS OR ALTERNATIVE TITLES ▼

PUBLICATION AS A CONTRIBUTION If this work was published as a contribution to a periodical, serial, or collection, give information about the collective work in which the contribution appeared. **Title of Collective Work ▼**

If published in a periodical or serial give: Volume ▼   Number ▼   Issue Date ▼   On Pages ▼

---

2 a
NAME OF AUTHOR ▼

DATES OF BIRTH AND DEATH
Year Born ▼   Year Died ▼

Was this contribution to the work a "work made for hire"?
☐ Yes
☐ No

AUTHOR'S NATIONALITY OR DOMICILE
Name of Country
OR { Citizen of ▶_____
Domiciled in ▶_____

WAS THIS AUTHOR'S CONTRIBUTION TO THE WORK
Anonymous?   ☐ Yes ☐ No
Pseudonymous? ☐ Yes ☐ No
If the answer to either of these questions is "Yes," see detailed instructions.

NOTE

Under the law, the "author" of a "work made for hire" is generally the employer, not the employee (see instructions). For any part of this work that was "made for hire" check "Yes" in the space provided, give the employer (or other person for whom the work was prepared) as "Author" of that part, and leave the space for dates of birth and death blank.

NATURE OF AUTHORSHIP Briefly describe nature of the material created by this author in which copyright is claimed. ▼

b
NAME OF AUTHOR ▼

DATES OF BIRTH AND DEATH
Year Born ▼   Year Died ▼

Was this contribution to the work a "work made for hire"?
☐ Yes
☐ No

AUTHOR'S NATIONALITY OR DOMICILE
Name of country
OR { Citizen of ▶_____
Domiciled in ▶_____

WAS THIS AUTHOR'S CONTRIBUTION TO THE WORK
Anonymous?   ☐ Yes ☐ No
Pseudonymous? ☐ Yes ☐ No
If the answer to either of these questions is "Yes," see detailed instructions.

NATURE OF AUTHORSHIP Briefly describe nature of the material created by this author in which copyright is claimed. ▼

c
NAME OF AUTHOR ▼

DATES OF BIRTH AND DEATH
Year Born ▼   Year Died ▼

Was this contribution to the work a "work made for hire"?
☐ Yes
☐ No

AUTHOR'S NATIONALITY OR DOMICILE
Name of Country
OR { Citizen of ▶_____
Domiciled in ▶_____

WAS THIS AUTHOR'S CONTRIBUTION TO THE WORK
Anonymous?   ☐ Yes ☐ No
Pseudonymous? ☐ Yes ☐ No
If the answer to either of these questions is "Yes," see detailed instructions.

NATURE OF AUTHORSHIP Briefly describe nature of the material created by this author in which copyright is claimed. ▼

3
YEAR IN WHICH CREATION OF THIS WORK WAS COMPLETED This information must be given in all cases.
◀ Year

DATE AND NATION OF FIRST PUBLICATION OF THIS PARTICULAR WORK
Complete this information ONLY if this work has been published.
Month ▶_____ Day ▶_____ Year ▶_____
◀ Nation

4
COPYRIGHT CLAIMANT(S) Name and address must be given even if the claimant is the same as the author given in space 2.▼

See instructions before completing this space.

TRANSFER If the claimant(s) named here in space 4 are different from the author(s) named in space 2, give a brief statement of how the claimant(s) obtained ownership of the copyright.▼

APPLICATION RECEIVED

ONE DEPOSIT RECEIVED

TWO DEPOSITS RECEIVED

REMITTANCE NUMBER AND DATE

DO NOT WRITE HERE OFFICE USE ONLY

MORE ON BACK ▶ • Complete all applicable spaces (numbers 5-11) on the reverse side of this page.
• See detailed instructions.   • Sign the form at line 10.

DO NOT WRITE HERE
Page 1 of_____pages

Application for Copyright (Front Cover)

NOTE: Card numbers cannot be preassigned to books which are already published.

DATE:_____

PUBLISHER'S NAME ON TITLE PAGE: _____

CONTACT PERSON:_____ PHONE NUMBER:_____

Type or print clearly the complete address to which the preassigned card number should be sent.
(This will be your return mailing label.)

	FOR CIP OFFICE USE
⌐ ⌐	Library of Congress Catalog Card Number preassigned is:
L ⌐	

Transcribe the information in items 1-6 exactly in the form and order in which it will appear on the title or copyright pages of the printed book. Use only those abbreviations which will actually appear on these pages. (Please attach a copy of the proposed title page, if available.)

1. Author(s) _____

2. Editor(s) _____

3. Title and subtitle(s) _____

_____

4. Edition statement (exactly as printed in the publication, e.g. second edition, revised edition, etc.) _____

_____

5. U.S. place of publication: City _____ State _____

Any copublisher (s) and place _____

6. Other information found on title page _____

_____

7. Series title (s) and numbering, exactly as printed in the publication _____

_____

8. Approximate number of pages _____ No. of volumes _____

9. ISBN _____ Binding: ☐ Hardcover ☐ Paperback

10. Proposed date of publication: Month _____ Year _____

11. Does (or will) the title in item 3 appear at periodic intervals, e.g. annually, quarterly, etc? ☐ Yes ☐ No

12. Will this publication be submitted later for CIP data? ☐ Yes ☐ No

For each title which receives a preassigned LC catalog card number, the Library of Congress requires one copy of the best edition of the published book. If selected for the Library's collections, the book will be cataloged. A postage-free, self-addressed label will be sent with the preassigned card number for your convenience in mailing the required advance copy of the work as soon as printed. This copy is in addition to copyright deposit copies.

Send this form to: **Library of Congress**
Cataloging in Publication Division
Washington, D.C. 20540

FOR CIP OFFICE USE ONLY.   DO NOT WRITE BELOW THIS LINE

Searching notes:

	RECD:
	ASGN:
607-7 (rev 2/84)	SENT:
	APIF:

Request for Library of Congress Catalog Card Number

INTERNATIONAL STANDARD BOOK NUMBERING. UNITED STATES AGENCY.
The International Numbering System in Publishing, Distribution and Library Practices
for Books, Software, Mixed Media, and other Education and Information Products.
205 East Forty-second Street, New York, New York 10017   212-916-1800

R.R. Bowker • The Information Company • A Division of Reed Publishing U.S.A.

<u>**APPLICATION FOR ISBN PUBLISHERS PREFIX**</u>
for books, Microforms, Mixed Media
Publications, including Video Tapes,
cassettes, & Microcomputer Software
<u>**PRINT OR TYPE**</u>

In order to assign the ISBN PUBLISHER PREFIX to your firm, we require the following:

WHAT IS YOUR PUBLISHING COMPANY NAME?_____
ADDRESS:_____CITY:_____ST.____ZIP:_____
IF P. O. BX, YOUR STREET ADDRESS IS REQUIRED_____

1. Year you started publishing   _____
2. Number of titles published in 1984   _____
3. Number of titles published in 1985   _____
4. Number of titles planned for 1986   _____   **YOUR CATALOG AND PROMOTION**
5. Number of titles you plan to do yearly _____ **MATERIALS ARE REQUIRED**
6. Number of titles still available (backlist) _____
7. Are you a Sub./Div. of another company?_____ Give name, address and ISBN Prefix:_____
_____
8. Do you have other publishing subsidiaries/imprints in the U.S. or foreign country? _____
   Give name, address, ISBN Prefix: _____
9. Do you distribute for any U.S./foreign publisher?_____Give name (s), address (es) and
   ISBN Prefix: _____
10. Are you distributed or represented by another company in the U.S. or foreign country?_____
    Give name (s), address (es) _____

Name your Office Staff ISBN Coordinator:_____
President/Director:_____
Your Phone number: __(___)_____   DATE:_____

Sincerely,

E Koltay

Emery Koltay, Director

    P.S. When our form is returned, we will assign an ISBN publisher prefix and send you
          a block of ISBN.

SAN - Standard Address Numbering   Out-of-State, Call toll free 1-800-247-7004

Director: Emery I. Koltay • Coordinator: Beatrice Jacobson • Officers: Melanie C. Walton, Isaura Perez, Peter Simon, Ernest Lee

Request for ISBN

ADVANCE BOOK INFORMATION

☐ Please keep last copy for your files
and return others when requested to: 47516

TITLE:

SERIES:

Original Title, if any:

Foreign Language: Translation ☐, from what language:

 AUTHOR(S):

EDITOR(S):

TRANSLATOR(S):

ILLUSTRATOR(S):

INTRO. BY; PREFACE BY; etc.

ILLUSTRATIONS (KIND & NUMBER).

PAGES:

AUDIENCE: Adult Layman ☐, (Also suitable for Young Adults? ☐)

Adult Professional ☐   College Text ☐

Elhi Text ☐: Grade: Juvenile ☐: Grade

Original Paperback ☐

Revised ☐   Abridged ☐   2nd Ed. ☐   Other:

 PUBLICATION DATE:
Reprint ☐: If reprint, name of orig. publisher & orig. pub. date:

 ENTER PRICE(S) BELOW: INT'L. STANDARD BOOK NUMBER
On short discount (20% or less) ☐

HARDCOVER TRADE: _ _._ _   ISBN _ _ _ _ _ _ _ _ _ _

If juv., is binding guaranteed?

LIBRARY BINDING: _ _._ _   ISBN _ _ _ _ _ _ _ _ _ _

HARDCOVER TEXT: _ _._ _   ISBN _ _ _ _ _ _ _ _ _ _

PAPER TRADE   _ _._ _   ISBN _ _ _ _ _ _ _ _ _ _

PAPER TEXT: _ _._ _   ISBN _ _ _ _ _ _ _ _ _ _

TCHRS. ED..   _ _._ _   ISBN _ _ _ _ _ _ _ _ _ _

WKBK: _ _._ _   ISBN _ _ _ _ _ _ _ _ _ _

LAB MANUAL.   _ _._ _   ISBN _ _ _ _ _ _ _ _ _ _

OTHER: SPECIFY   _ _._ _   ISBN _ _ _ _ _ _ _ _ _ _

LC #

Order # (optional):

| FOR INTERNAL USE ONLY |
| PUB. |
| IMPR. |

PUBLISHER:

Address

DISTRIBUTOR, if other than publisher:

IMPRINT:

Appendix ☐   Bibliography ☐   Footnotes ☐
Index ☐   Other:

Programmed Book ☐

Reissue ☐   New Edition ☐   First U.S. Edition ☐

Import ☐. If yes, are you exclusive distributor?

Simultaneous cloth & paper publication ☐   Talking Book ☐

BRIEF DESCRIPTION OF BOOK

AUTHOR/EDITOR/ILLUS. BIOGRAPHICAL INFORMATION:

ADVERTISING, PROMOTION & PUBLICITY PLANS:

SUBJECT CATEGORY:

ISBN NOTE. If you assign your own ISBNs, put full 10 digit number in spaces above. The system requires a separate ISBN for each edition.

Completed by: _____

Listing Form for *Books In Print,* Etc. (See Page 27)